W9-AHJ-802

BIG SPIRITS, LITTLE BODIES

BIG SPIRITS, LITTLE BODIES

PARENTING YOUR WAY TO WHOLENESS

by Linda Crispell Aronson

A.R.E. Press • Virginia Beach • Virginia

Copyright © 1995
by Linda Crispell Aronson

1st Printing, June 1995

Printed in the U.S.A.

All rights reserved. No part of this book may be reproduced
or transmitted in any form or by any means, electronic or
mechanical, including photocopying, recording or by any
information storage and retrieval system, without permis-
sion in writing from the Publisher.

A.R.E. Press
Sixty-Eighth & Atlantic Avenue
P.O. Box 656
Virginia Beach, VA 23451-0656

Library of Congress Cataloging-in-Publication Data
Aronson, Linda Crispell 1953-
    Big spirits, little bodies : parenting your way to wholeness / by
Linda Crispell Aronson.
        p.   cm.
    Includes bibliographical references.
    ISBN 0-87604-337-6
    1. Parenting. I. Title.
HQ755.8.A73   1995
649'.1—dc20   95-5156

Cover design by Richard Boyle

Dedication

For My Beloved Family, Dick, Toby, and Angela—
we did it together.

Contents

Acknowledgments

To Dick Aronson, who became a super-parent and super-spouse while I worked at the computer or in my head and who gave me the courage and safety to create, through his untamed love and steadfast support, inch by inch.

To Toby Aronson, who exuberantly recited the growing list of chapters as I wrote them and who came to understand that I love to write like he loves football.

To Angela Aronson, for her company and her magnificent drawings that inspired me as I worked and for asking me if I was going to give my computer a valentine on February 14, 1993.

To my mother and father, who were always ahead of their time in many ways; one of the greatest was in parenting.

To Diane Harlowe, who shares my love of creating and who supported me with her loving and generous spirit every stage and step of the way.

To my editor, Ken Skidmore, who called me every week for eleven months, listened to my ups and downs, made me laugh when I got too serious, and gave my book a high compliment: "It makes me want to go out and rent some kids."

To legendary writer and professor Marshall Cook, who said four magic words, "You can do it." He knew because he taught me how.

To A.R.E. Press, who said, "We want your book."

To Betsy Saar, who always asked, "How is the book?" and who intuited my need for support at several hard spots along the way.

To Diane Nuttycombe, who took exquisite care of my children while I wrote in the early mornings.

To Ann Rapaleye Shoemaker, Diana Rian, Laurel Deegan Finn, and Alissa Bratz, for the loving spirit you showered on my children.

To Molly Allison, who lighted up when I shared my dream; I then knew it had a life.

To literary agent Nancy Love, who absolutely loved my book and knew its time had come.

To my bonus parents, in random order: Mrs. Cape, Mrs. Kelsey, Mr. Starna, Mr. Struglia, Mr. Jackson, Mrs. Johnson, Mrs. Fitzgibbons, Dr. McNary, Mr. Berman, Virginia Light, Dr. Casey, Professor Betty Boller, David Smith, Susan Carey, Katie Tobey, Fred Turner, Bob Green, Philip Fried, Brian Williams, Donald Smith, Professor Martha Knight, Shirley Meirers, Sarah Sadd, Grandma Nellie, and the ones I have forgotten in face or name.

To Dr. David Elkind, for granting an interview and articulating my deep-down beliefs.

To Rue Ann Hass, who generously dropped off her proposal in my mailbox one day when I needed to see one; she must know I am a visual learner.

To Adele Faber, who set me afire when she came to Madison.

To the musicmakers who regenerated my spirit: Gregory Norbet, Raffi, and Tom Pease.

To the writers who fed me when I was on empty: Madeleine L'Engle, Wallace Stegner, Marianne Williamson, Natalie Goldberg, Clarissa Pinkola Estes, and Sophy Burnham.

To Robert Fritz, for teaching me the "secrets" of creating.

To New Dimensions Radio and The Institute of Noetic Sciences, for your weekly inspiration and higher vision for humanity that kept me writing.

FOREWORD

I CAN REMEMBER being a big spirit in a little body. I had an inner voice that spoke to me, not in words but awareness. I saw more light and color then; everything was brilliant. Nothing was separate from anything else. Nothing was bad nor good. There was no fear. All I knew was trust. I was very, very young. Then I grew up. Gradually my inner voice quieted. I learned to see things as separate, and when I started to see myself as separate, I experienced fear for the first time. All the bright lights and colors faded. What changed? I did. I was shifting out of spirit into the body of life in the world.

The first two decades of life are dedicated to the maturation of body and brain. That is the way it should be, a total immersion in growth and development. During that time my mind absorbed the prevailing beliefs about reality. I learned about my time and culture. Gradually, I learned how to survive in this world. But deep down inside, I knew there was more to me, the world, and beyond. I knew that a human being was more than a body and brain I had dissected in anatomy lab. I knew that the mind and heart together could heal the body and soul. I knew there was a purpose to our spin in the universe. And I knew children had more light, were closer to truth and easier with their love than adults.

As a child, I learned that you get a spirit after you die. But as I grew older, I heard another view. You do not get a spirit after you die, because you already have a spirit and always did. But what does a spirit do? What is it good for? If I don't need one in life, why would I need one after? By the time I reached adulthood, my interest in and curiosity about spirit were growing more intense. I picked my profession, occupational therapy, because its philosophy was holistic, integrating the mind, body, and spirit in the process of healing. I was curious about spirit but conservative and cautious. Sources had to be "credible." I was obliged. My college roommate, who was majoring in medical technology, taught me to see auras. I learned to meditate concurrent with taking a course on the different states of consciousness while I was at Tufts University. While doing clinical training at a major medical center, I learned about extra-physical healing from a member of the medical staff. Later, I learned about all kinds of spiritual phenomena from none other than an attorney.

Everything I learned thrilled me. I felt my own spirit stirring—that part of me I had put to bed in order to grow up. I didn't even have to die first! My spirit was dusty, out of practice, in dire need of exercise and polishing like an instrument that had sat in the attic for twenty years. My regenerating spirit spawned some mind-expanding experiences, but they were still primarily intellectual. If I was going to do anything with my re-found spirit, I needed a practice, something that committed me on a daily basis whether I felt like it or not. I wanted to exercise my spirit, put it to work, test it to the limit, ground it in everyday life, root it in the physical. Then I became a parent. My search was over.

Parenting is pregnant with opportunities to return to our spirit and grow whole again, mind, body, and spirit. Our children are catalysts for growing whole. They are big spirits in little bodies. Parents have big bodies and minds with quiescent spirits.

Many people view parenting and personal growth as conflicting areas. My book takes another view. I call it the "other side of parenting," the side where the parent is growing, growing toward wholeness by recovering the spirit he or she left behind in order to grow up. In essence, parenting is a growth spurt of the spirit.

Today's parents are special. Many of us are raising our children in the second half of our lives, the midlife years, the season of spiritual questing. I believe the evolution of parenting to this stage of life reaches beyond the postponement of children for career. Parenting has climbed into the laps of midlifers so that we can embrace it as part of our spiritual quest.

At the time I was first playing with the idea of writing one book about my two passions, parenting and spirit, I joined a friend on impulse and attended an open meditation meeting. For that night's meditation, we were to meet our spiritual guide and ask for guidance on some matter in our lives. I asked for help with shaping the vision for my book. My guide, a woman of layered light, stood before me and took out one of her eyes and then took out one of her teeth. She put them both into her hand, stretched out her arm, and offered them to me. After the meditation, I told the facilitator about my experience and asked about the symbolism of the eye and the tooth. She said, "Hmmm, an eye and a tooth, an eye and a tooth ... an eyetooth! Let me do some research and I'll get back to you." Several days later she called, very excited. "Linda, I've got some information on the eyetooth. I talked to my husband, who is a dentist; he said the eyetooth is between the incisors and the bicuspids in the upper jaw. It is the pointed tooth that cuts deeply and has the deepest roots. The root of the eyetooth is connected to all the other roots of the teeth." "Ah, now I get it," I said. "To cut deeply ... to see deeply ... down to the roots."

So that is how my book was conceived—by an eyetooth. Creating the book was a process of writing, writing, writing my way down to the root to illuminate the gifts of spirit our children bring to us and the opportunity parenting holds for growing whole by reclaiming our own spirit. In essence, *BIG SPIRITS, Little Bodies* is a book of illumination, a "how to see" book.

It was my intention that *BIG SPIRITS, Little Bodies* would inspire or jump right out and make love to the reading parent, both the personal parent—the caregiver of his or her own children—and the generic parent, or anyone who nurtures children of all ages. I once heard a dear friend say in a speech before an audience of five hundred therapists, "I need lots of inspiration in my life to function at my best." I thought to myself, "Ditto." It is no less true, maybe more so, for parents. Where do we get inspiration? It comes from the spirit.

The book can be read in short snatches of time, and it is therefore compatible with the life-style of the all-too-busy parent. I have tried to make it a lively and easy read. True to the theme of the book, the chapters are whole in themselves so you can skip around.

All the anecdotes are true, but almost all the names and descriptive details have been changed. The world is a small place. I hope to avoid having my friends bump into each other in my book. I also wish to honor the privacy and privilege of our shared lives.

Spiritual questing, growing whole, and parenting belong to one another. They are intrinsically connected. Growth in any one venture cross-fertilizes the others. They all take inner strength, stamina for the long stretch, and complete commitment. Growth is not often smooth or easy. It is bumpy. (My pet name for parenting is "bumpy bliss.") A mother of three once told me, while reviewing her less-than-peaceful vacation, "I have to keep reminding myself when my children argue with each other or me, 'Oh, yes, this is growth.'" We laughed. Tribulations go with the territory. We will be tested over and over again. And we will be rewarded for our growth with moments of magnificence, boundless love, transcendent tenderness, surges into big spirit, and, of course, greater wholeness.

Part I

====

Bumpy Bliss

1

THE GREAT SURRENDER

O N A W H I M , I decided to show off Upper Buttermilk Falls to my children. We had already had a full day at the lake, but it was a luscious day in mid-June, one of those most-beautiful-days-of-the-whole-year. Just the name *Buttermilk* sent a ricochet of delight throughout my body, a sensation I could still feel from childhood. I had not been there in twenty years. I wanted to share it with my children and see if it still played its magic on me.

The waterfall was full and the noise deafening. The mist tingled my skin and swept the new green smell in the air.

The rocky creek below had pools of deep water, and the current was strong. The bank was steep and filled with large boulders with openings to trap small feet. I watched my six-year-old son as he scampered around looking for rocks to throw into the whirlpool below. It was shaded dark from the sedimentary rock and overhanging trees above. I had my hawkeye on him, since he was a non-swimmer. The roar of the falls drowned my warnings to my son to get away from the water's edge. With a tired back and a body that had swirled children in water all day at the lake, I trailed down the rock after him. I was able to guide him back without protest, under the pretense that I had something to show him.

When we got to the top, I quickly surveyed the landscape to find something to show him that was worthy of personal escort. Barely holding off his impatient demand of "What? ... WHAT!!," I headed along down the top of the bank.

Peering into the shallow, clear water below, I hunted among polished stones. The water rippled across the rocks now, the current calming. The pockets of water scattered here and there were no more than a foot or so deep. Finally I spotted them, small minnows. I pointed for my son to see. It wasn't long before he had water gushing out the sides of his sneakers. He looked up at me in full grin. The minnows were forgotten. My son was headed downstream. I looked at the small pools ahead, and then I looked down at my own feet. Could I spare these slip-on shoes that had taken on the contours of my feet? My effort was halfhearted, as I tried to step from rock to rock surveying the stream for dry stones. Before long my shoes were gushing, too. We slipped and slid on the mossy rocks. Whoops! I was in and I was wet, all wet. We splashed each other silly. With the current running at our heels, we headed downstream, together.

That is how parents surrender. We are pulled in. We get wet.

Getting wet can be a real shock. When new moms and dads talk of what parenting has done to them, we hear pejorative wails. Oh, the sleepless nights, the burden of fatigue, the constant demands, the loss of grown-up privacy, the interruptions, the hassles, the chaos. We are thrashing in the water, reaching in desperation for solid ground. To surrender is to bob in the incoming waves, to be carried by the tides. When we become parents, life dissolves into its essence; the excess is all washed away. Losses are inevitable. Friends will drift away, careers will seem to erode, your life will sting as it scrapes the sandy bottom in the undertow.

We pull back. We pull back from deep water, not because we fear that our child will be lost in the big, dark pool, but because we fear that *we* will be lost. Our children startle us by throwing a rock in the reflecting pool so that our image is jagged and broken. We are cracked wide open. There is so much that wants to possess us: power, prestige, profession. There is so little that calls us into the water—little, but powerful—our children. Our children pull us in with a force that has deep currents, deep enough to knock us off our feet and send us tumbling into the breakwater. We can no longer stand on firm ground. We fear that we will lose ground. But water will seep in anyway. It can drip, trickle, babble, rush, and roar. It is our children who pull us in, into the flow of life.

To surrender into parenting is to be like children learning to swim. Our first reaction is often fear—fear that the water will not hold us up and we will drown. There is a lot of resistance. It is okay to get our bodies in the water as long as we can touch the bottom and we don't have to get our faces wet. We think we can sneak. We will just hold our heads out of the water and do the dog paddle—the pseudostroke. But we have to stop to wipe our faces off every time we get splashed. We cannot venture out very far or very deep.

Perhaps it is too many lessons, or peer pressure, or maybe it is the allure of deeper water, diving for rings, underwater somersaults and handstands, or jumping off the diving board, that finally works. The child surrenders and puts his face in, gets wet, lets the water drip down the forehead, around the ears, and in the eyes.

Once we are all in, totally wet, then we can finally maneuver in water, learn the strokes, tread in deep water, dive to the bottom, and build our endurance for the long distance swim of parenting.

To surrender into parenting is to submerge into life, to leave dry ground. Water is precious in the galactic sense. It has not been found in abundance anywhere else in the solar system. The closest water planet may be light years away, or nowhere. Life is held in water. Water brings life—male and female moistures merge—sperm spurts into wet wombs. Life is wet.

Surrendering is a secret practice of parenting, to be learned over and over again: getting off the phone, collapsing on the floor to read a book, forgetting that last errand, being home most nights, developing child/parent rituals and language, sharing your days and your dreams.

Surrendering is not giving up or giving in. It is not sacrifice. It is giving forth, releasing our children like spawn into the stream of life. To parent is to keep the stream clear of debris that will block the flow. It is to guide our children around the big rocks and boulders. It is to show them a clear reflection. It is to splash when the water is calm and shallow and be a buoy when the current is too strong or the water too deep. To parent is to pull them out of the water from time to time and let them rest on dry ground for a while.

To surrender into parenting is to dive deeper into life than we ever have before. On the surface, we find everything from buggy joggers to "toilet training in one day." Way down deep, waiting for us at the bottom, if we dare make the dive, we can find the missing stones to our own wholeness. Our children threw them into the water, but it is up to us to retrieve them. To surrender into parenting is to get wet so that we can make the deep dive into life.

You know you are surrendering when:
• You see your life with your child as your real life and the world you share together as the real world.

- You want to participate in your child's life and your child wants to participate in your life.
- You respect your child as much as or more than any adult.
- You truly enjoy your child's companionship.
- You want to take the very best care of yourself for your child.
- You know that parenting is the most important and far-reaching work you will do in your life.

2

SHEDDING

DRIZZLE AND DAMP. I felt a chill as I sat by the window nursing my newborn. It was early spring and early day, six in the morning. Snowfall dusted the ground, a great discouragement after six months of winter. The day before, the sun had been in and out. Winds blew the dried leaves of last fall around, mixed with a hint of spring. Spring is like birth; it doesn't come easy. Fall, winter, and summer just come, but spring must be born. There can be setbacks and false hopes. Spring can try our patience; we wonder if the new life will ever come. It always seems that just as we give up, stop struggling against nature, and let go, then it happens: the baby is born, and spring comes.

After weeks of Lamaze training, huffing and puffing breathing exercises, positive affirmations, praying, and visualizations, our baby came the hard way: twenty-four hours of hard labor, three hours of pushing, and major surgery to open my womb. I sat in my chair by the window, with my baby in my arms, feeling my life was over—and it was. I remember thinking, "My life will never be the same again"—and it hasn't been. I remember feeling like I was dying (considering what I had been through, maybe I was!) in the sense that life, now my old life, was going to unravel—and it did. I felt like I was shedding as the animal sheds its winter coat in spring. It was as if I had lost a protective layer of skin. I was more sensitive to smells, light, sound, motion.

To be born, to live and breathe in this world, a child must shed its mother's womb, the placenta, amniotic sac, and umbilical cord. To care for, nurture, and raise a child, the newborn parent must shed, too.

Not long after I had been taken out of my birthing room and into the labor room, an orderly called from the other side of the curtain, "Linda Aronson has a phone call." It was from the school board, of which I was a member. The board was stalemated on a critical vote. They needed my vote to break the tie. They had already checked with their attorney to see if the board, all twelve members, could come to the hospital for the vote. No go. My attending nurse snapped back at the orderly without turning her attention from me, "She can't take a call—she's having a baby!" He persisted, "They want to know if there is any way she could just come down the hill and across the street for the vote—it would just take a minute." The nurse looked at me with wild, unbelieving eyes. "My God, what do those people think?" She swirled around and shouted at the orderly behind the curtain, "No! I said she was having a baby, *right now!*"

Birth interrupts our lives, it interrupts the lives of others; it is hard to let go, it is hard for everyone to let go, and that is just the beginning.

Four weeks later, I did manage to get to a board meeting; I was still in a fog and flying high with postpartum euphoria. I remember thinking how rambling all their discussions and how petty their disagreements seemed to me now. I thought to myself, "And I used to be really into this, right in the middle of it all!" More dying. I sat there watching their mouths move, but not listening. Some questioned my silence, but several senior and seasoned mothers just left me alone, giving me a knowing smile.

Shedding is like a giant growth spurt. When children go through growth spurts, they disintegrate for a period of time; they regress. So do parents. The disintegration is necessary for the new structure, or complexity, to take place. You can't just add new growth on top of the old structure. It just won't work; it won't hold up. The old needs to come apart, to come tumbling down before the new, more complex organization and form can take shape.

To become a parent is to shed an old skin that is too tight, too confining. You are growing, and your old skin just doesn't fit anymore. For reptiles and birds, it is called molting: *replaced by new growth*. I can remember the summer I saw the molted skin of a snake out the back steps of our new home. Since I was six years old at the time, I was very curious about this phenomenon. I could not understand how our adopted snake could get along without his skin. How did he get out of it? Did it hurt? Was he okay? Did he die and was this what was left of his body? The fact was, he had just outgrown his old skin.

Flexible Skin:

A parent needs a skin that is more elastic, stretchy, and flexible than the old one. We will be pulled and stretched in all directions, and we need that extra flexibility. The places where we are rigid are where we will crack first. I am a pretty flexible person, but I need my sleep, and lots of it, nine to ten hours a night to feel my absolute best. When I had a colicky infant who wanted to nurse every half hour around the clock, I thought I would go mad from sleep deprivation.

So I went against traditional child-rearing advice and brought my babe to bed with us. It saved my sanity. As for my husband, he cracks not under pressure but under clutter. For him, chaos is toxic. But with small children, a parent can become a pick-up machine and not do much else. So we decided to quarantine one area from clutter, our bedroom, so that my husband could find sanctuary in his own home, one space to go to restore his sanity.

As children grow, you can never go back to the way things were. You cannot return to your rigid ways when you dispose of the very last diaper. You have to constantly invent new rules that fit your new reality. Seven years into parenting, I lost it one Christmas when my son insisted upon opening up packages from relatives as U.P.S. delivered them at the door. "We wait until Christmas!" I yelled. Now that's the spirit, mom. Humbug. The next year, I let the children open the packages as they arrived. It spread out their fun over the holidays, and they remembered and enjoyed the gifts more than if they had been stashed under the tree and opened all at once.

People enter parenting with varying degrees of flexibility. Some flexible souls seem to fold parenting right into their lives, and others need to limber up.

One scholarly mother joked that her home had replaced piles of books and academic paraphernalia with piles of laundry, "One pile for each day of the week," she said. "At least with dirty laundry, it doesn't matter if you step on it." The contents changed, but the structure remains the same. "Actually," she continued, "these piles are a blessing; on the days when I feel like I get nothing done—other than nursing—if I manage to put in a load or two, I can see the fruits of my labor. It doesn't seem to matter what I'm doing," she chuckled. "I guess I like to pile my life high."

Faye maintains her flexibility in the water. Swimming was like breathing to her. When she had her baby, she did not give up swimming, but she had to make some changes.

First, she wanted to find a pool that would allow her to bring her stroller on the deck. She swam for an hour while the baby slept. When the baby got older and no longer napped in the early morning, she sat him up in the stroller and attached a tray for shaking and mouthing toys. Faye did the backstroke down the pool and the breaststroke back to keep her eye on him. He squealed with delight when she returned to his end of the pool, as she lunged up at him or splashed him ever so lightly. Then he would wait for the next round. It was a game. After the swim, mother and baby showered together, skin to skin. They rubbed down with lotion and towel.

It wasn't long before there were three or four strollers at the end of each lane for mid-morning swims. One morning I asked Faye about her swims. She said, "When I swim first thing in the morning, I can really give myself to my son, I have the energy, and I am not always in conflict about his needs versus my needs. But mine must come first. It's as if he instinctively knows that, and he gives me the time." Faye's approach reminded me of the standard emergency procedure on planes: "If traveling with a small child, put your own oxygen mask on first before assisting your child."

Transparent Skin:

In addition to flexible skin, a parent also needs transparent skin: showing on the outside what you are on the inside. Skin was not meant to be a shield to hide behind; it was meant to be a gentle covering, a sensual organ, the place of contact, touching, and caressing. When we touch the utter delicacy of our newborn baby's skin, our own skin softens. We molt our hardened layer. In the process of growing up, we have learned to hide behind our skin. We use our skin as a barrier that separates our inside self from our outside self. We learn to tuck away both vulnerability and sensitivity under the skin.

My friend John, a gifted songwriter and musician now in

his sixties, is transparent. I don't know whether he has always been that way or if he turned transparent later in life. I remember he asked me once, "Why is it that people are most attractive when they are vulnerable?" He did not mean in terms of physical beauty or sex appeal, but rather that when a person is vulnerable, the authenticity attracts you, you are drawn to him, you step out of your own skin and dare to touch his skin, to make contact, human being to human being.

Children are very transparent, at least for the first several years, and then around age five they start to button up and sew up the seams of their skin. When a child is vulnerable—bumps his head, is lost in a store, breaks a favorite toy, is afraid of the clown—we reflexively tend to him. We do not hesitate. We are wholehearted in our care. I remember thinking, during my son's colic and my sleep deprivation, "There is no one else in the world I could do this for." I meant it literally. I do not believe I would have physically been able to do it for anyone else.

It is necessary and appropriate that at times we cover up, do not let others see our vulnerabilities or see through us. We have learned this so well that it is hard to do otherwise, to switch into transparency. But a parent needs to be transparent. I learned this lesson when my son, between the ages of three and four, asked me from time to time, "Are you my mother?" At first, I was bewildered by this question. Then I remembered the development of imagination and the picture book *Are You My Mother?* by P. D. Eastman about the little bird who hatches, falls out of his nest, and goes around the barnyard asking, "Are you my mother?" to all the animals. I thought my son had heard it at preschool, on "Sesame Street," or at a friend's house. But no, he had never heard of the story. Then I thought that perhaps this was a cute way of getting my attention, a kind of game, so I played along. "Oh, no, I am the ostrich's mother," I said. My son appreciated my attempt at humor and tried to laugh along, but it was a half laugh and half cry. He persisted, "Are you my mommy?" What was this? Some magical thinking of preschoolers, too many fairy tales, the fallout of instant transformation seen in cartoons? Finally I asked him, "Why do you ask me that?" "Because you don't seem like my mommy," he said. Then I got cued in—I must seem different to him for some reason. I checked myself over, looking for new makeup, hair, or clothing. Nothing there.

Then, after some reflection, I finally got it. My son had exposed a rule I hadn't even known I was following. I didn't even know where I got it or who had made it up. There's the rule: A good parent is a perfect person. (You've got to be kidding!) A perfect person does not express negative feelings. (Says who?) So, in my attempt to follow this subterfuge rule, I tried to be perfect according to the rule's misguidance. So when negativity was around, I became a perfectly phony parent.

My son saw through my act, and it troubled him. It wasn't that he wanted a mother who was the all-time-perfect-person-parent with no ruffles, but that he needed a mother who was real. So I zapped the triple "P" (perfect parent person) rule and let some "negatives" leak out in small doses: "Oh, I am so tired; I'm getting really crabby; Darn it all! I need a break; Grrrr, I can't get this to work; I hate to cook; I like laundry even less; I'll go crazy if . . . " My son delights in these infirmities. They put him at ease. What he senses and the way I act are in sync. Of course, I spare him the details. He doesn't care about them anyway. He just wants me to be the way he knows I am. It is clearer. Transparency builds trust in a parent-child relationship.

Shedding "Perfect"

So to be a better parent, I had to shed "perfect." I had always told myself, "If I can't do it perfectly, I don't want to do it at all." Two of my "perfect" areas were teaching and entertaining. By holding out for "perfect," I was stalled. After my baby was born, I did not have the time or energy, so I thought, to entertain or work up classes to my own standards. So I starved myself of both for a time, until my friend Mary saved me. Once when I was lamenting about my situation, Mary said, "You may not be able to do it perfectly, but you can sure do a great job!" I got her point.

"Perfect" can get in the way of all kinds of wonderful things. For instance, the question of "dog or no dog" is a recurring discussion in both my friend Barbara's and my family. She and I both knew who would end up caring for the family dog in our respective families. Mom. We both hesitated to bring one more responsibility into our already too-full lives. Barbara sighed, "Having a dog would be one more relationship that I wouldn't do perfectly."

Some people know how to be perfectly imperfect. My friend Ellen does not have two dishes that match, yet all her place settings fit together perfectly. She does not stop at the dishes; her linen napkins are all different colors, the chairs to her table are different styles, and the furniture in her home is of different woods. It is all on purpose, and it works perfectly. Ellen graces you with comfort and ease in both her presence and her home. She is the perfect hostess. So now instead of entertaining, I think of *hosting*, in the spirit of Ellen.

Dropping "perfect" has made me a better teacher too. Teaching is not about the perfect presentation or performance. It is about listening, facilitating, integrating, illuminating, synthesizing, and highlighting. In order to do that, I had to change positions as teacher. Instead of standing up in front, separate from the class, I now become part of the class. It is harder, but it is better.

We most definitely have to let go of our idea of the perfect child—no one has ever had one. They are simply not to be found, thank goodness! We all have an idea of what our children will be like, or at least we have our dreams. Many parents comment that their children are more wonderful than they ever could have imagined. When we try to push "perfect" on them, whether it be in the way they comb their hair, clean their room, or chew their food, they will do one of three things—react, recoil, or rebel. Pushing perfect as a parent is a waste of time. As literary agent Nancy Love, mother of two grown children, told me, "I finally realized that when my son discovered girls, then he would start combing his hair."

Shedding a Life

For today's parent who has developed a career before having children, becoming a parent may precipitate a crisis in identity. We are what we do.

Helen is a high achiever. She is in crisis over the loss of a career that she spent her twenties and thirties building. She is a research chemist and held a tenured faculty position at a prestigious university. She was in demand as a speaker at professional conferences. When she had her first child, she continued working. But when she had her second child, she dropped back to part-time. But it was still not enough. "This one is different from my first; she just could not tolerate the separation," said Helen. "I had an inner knowing that was very strong, it overpowered me, I hated being away from her, it was just awful, and it didn't make any sense. I loved going to work. What I was experiencing inside me and all the messages coming from the outside were in a head-on collision." Helen took a year's leave of absence. She feels what she did was right for her younger child, but she worries. "I will never be able to build what I had; I've almost accepted that. But now I wonder, 'Will there be a place for me when I return?' It is impossible to keep up with all the research now . . . I just don't know what will happen."

Human shedding is breaking out in new skin that is more flexible and transparent. It can leave us feeling insecure at times, not knowing what to do. Humans do not shed without pain, conflict, and confusion. It is different from the molting of reptiles or birds. Human shedding causes all kinds of shifting: values, habits, lifestyles, rules, personality, and identity. Shedding is hard work, part of the process of becoming a parent and a whole person.

3

SIZING UP SACRIFICE

I' M A B U M P E R reader. Bumper stickers can tell you a lot about a complete stranger. The "I'd rather be . . . " ones are my favorites: "I'd rather be dancing, I'd rather be fishing, I'd rather be biking, I'd rather be skiing, I'd rather be golfing, I'd rather be flying." How about "I'd rather be parenting?" Now that would be a real traffic-stopper. The only bumper sticker that would top that would have to be "I'd rather be living."

Parenting is just about the only occupation that you do not need a license to practice. For the most part, it goes completely unregulated. There are no continuing education requirements. No benefits either: no paid vacation, no social security, no health insurance, no annuity or pension, not to mention no salary. Parenting is lean on prestige and big on so-called "sacrifice."

Parenting is your longest-term project. It is the ultimate test of delayed gratification. Success comes in small packages: a sleeping child, a spontaneous hug, an eaten meal, tied shoes, writing one's name, making a friend, riding a bike. There are no promotions, no raises, no awards ceremonies or pins for service. The rewards are private; parents often experience them alone.

It's hard to sell this business of parenting. Parents are constantly tempted to sacrifice themselves and their children to false gods. The allures of power, prestige, wealth, and overachievement are everywhere. But parenting is not in the "getting" or "having" part of life. It is in the *being* part. It belongs to the growing in love and wisdom part. Until this is clear, parenting is a constant conflict in our lives.

We cannot *have* children; we can only share life with them. We all say, "I have a son; I have three children." What if we said, "I share my life with two sons and a daughter'? In the same way, making a child does not make a parent. A parent is something to *become* with experience and growth.

Does our commitment to our children have to be framed as sacrifice? Sacrifice, yes, if we want to live a status quo life. Sacrifice, no, if we embrace parenting as an opportunity to grow. A parent does not commit to the arduous work of parenting on the birth day of her child, once and for always. Parenting is like marriage; it is a series of recommitments made over time and circumstance. It is the *recommitment* that makes it a choice.

Parenting is often viewed as a regression. But that only works from the limited perspective of ego and materialism. When we fully embrace parenting, we are choosing another framework for our lives. Parenting can be a very vague and nonspecific profession. Each of us needs to reframe our lives so we can define and articulate, at least to ourselves, our role, our work, our purpose in parenting. The commitment to parenting forces us to identify and name, at least for ourselves, our bottom-line values. This clarity will give us a structure to build and shape our lives with our children and inform the multitudes of decisions and conflicts that we will face as parents.

The Great Parenting Shift

When I had my first child, I felt ripped down the middle, seared down the sternum and to the navel. I was divided in two, my old life on one side and my new life on the other. All of a sudden those things that I had "filled" my work life with—planning, meeting, organizing—seemed like, what can I say? . . . fill. But with my babe, I was at the epicenter of life. This new thing in my life, parenting, was exquisite, like the mist of a waterfall, the smell of jasmine, and the sound of deep breaths and steady heartbeats. Being a newborn parent brought me life I never knew before, never knew existed.

Reframing Our Lives

Cheryl Jarvis writes about her ten-year commitment to parenting as her primary occupation in a feisty commentary to the *Wall Street Journal:* "During those years, I learned to live with insecurity and fear . . . But for the first time in my life I became unafraid. I learned to live without a career identity and discovered that a successful life has little to do with the job titles and everything to do with relationships." So what was the return on her investment? "It was through raising them that I became an adult, through raising them that I forgave my parents, through raising them that I discovered what life is really about."[1]

Sylvia Ann Hewlett, economist and author of the best-selling book *When the Bough Breaks: The Cost of Neglecting Our Children,* left a teaching job at Barnard College to pursue a new career as an advocate for families and children. Hewlett writes, "I put my skills as an economist to work to convince policy-makers that children are one of the best investments this country can make." In 1993, she founded the National Parenting Association, an organization committed to spreading the word that raising children is much more than an expensive hobby. "It is one of the most rewarding things you can do for yourself and society," says Hewlett.[2]

Tracy Will sat on the stone wall of the Union Terrace. His wife, Gay, sat next to him, a toddler in her lap; a baby slept in a stroller. It was early April, and no one else was about. But I understood; I was there for the same reason. The parents of young children need a place to go. We are the early birds breaking out into spring, shaking off the cabin fever, putting our faces into the sun and the wind. Tracy had just completed his first book, *Wisconsin*, a tour guide of the state. Tracy and Gay eagerly told me of how the whole family drove all over the state doing research for his book. The whole project took nine months. The family endured many rough spots, but they were committed to seeing it through.

"Before we were parents, we lived the high life staying out at night," explained Gay. "I am an actress. Now that has all changed. We are home every night. You know, I don't really miss it either, which really surprises me. Ninety percent of evolution gears you for home life."

"Actually, I find parenting refreshing," put in Tracy. "Parenting is like drinking from the well of your soul."

Several months later, on a humid Friday evening in July, I saw Gay again at almost the same place, sitting on the stone wall, holding her babe next to the double stroller. This time the Terrace was swarming with people, and a band was blaring. I approached Gay. She lighted up and remembered me. I asked how *Wisconsin* was doing. "They can't keep it on the bookshelves," she beamed. "You know, Tracy almost gave it up so many times, and now we are glad he didn't. Now lots of people are taking the trip through the book that we took last year." I congratulated her. I told Gay that I had written about her family in my book and mentioned Tracy's quote about "drinking from the well." She said, "Actually, Tracy more often says parenting is like plumbing a *new* well into your soul." I thanked her for the edit. "I like that even better," I said.

Margaret is a lawyer. Years ago, I had several heart-to-heart talks with her about balancing career and parenting as our children played at a parent-tot program. Our daughters were a year apart and were preschoolers at that time. Margaret looked burdened, tired, torn. She painted a picture of her parenting experience as the referee of her daughters' sibling rivalry over Mom's attention. She was suffering from back pain and seeing a physical therapist. "I feel guilty about my girls when I'm at work, and I feel guilty about work when I am home." On the last day of the parent-tot program before summer break, she came up to tell me she was close to handing in her resignation. She seemed resigned herself, but certainly not resolved. She knew what she was about to give up, but not what she was getting.

Six months later, I saw her by chance at the mall during the holidays. As we brushed shoulders in the crowd, she said, "I did it, and so far I love it!" Her eyes were shining, and her shoulders had dropped, elongating her neck and opening up her face. Her movement had lightened. I wondered, "Is it just the holidays, is she doing yoga, or is it really her decision that made her change so much?"

A full year later we met again at the café of my neighborhood bookstore. She invited me to have coffee with her; she wanted to talk. She was struggling again, but it was not the either/or question; it was a question of finding balance. Before, she had been trying to figure out how to fit children into her life. Now she was trying to figure out how to fit work into her life. Margaret had traded in her power suits for sweat pants and Nikes. She had been freelancing with her law firm, working on special projects about ten hours a week. She was also volunteering at her daughter's school, and she had moved so her family could be in a more community-oriented environment. "My daughters have playmates over all the time. There are twenty-five kids at the bus stop. My kids are in heaven. For the first time, I feel like a real mother and a member of the community."

Still there was struggle. "Life seems to have become a stage," Margaret reflected. "Everyone wants to be rich and famous, we want to leave behind a legacy, our mark, we are always asking, 'What am I about? What do I want to say about me?' We want to be big people in the world . . . it is the media thing, we all want to get on TV. It is not enough anymore to be a big person in one's own community, neighborhood, school, or church. People have lost that connection, that kind of identity, and are looking for it on the world stage." She was sifting through her values, perhaps saying good-bye to the dreams of her ideal. Shifting is never easy. The "what-ifs" always linger.

Continuous Challenge

My friend Mary was having dinner with her husband's work associates. They asked her what she was going to do now that both her children were in school. "They just don't get it. If you have not had a hands-on parenting experience, it is hard to explain. Every time I consider what I might want to do in the adult world, I think, 'I can do that.' But parenting is always a challenge. I have worked through so much stuff being a parent. As a result, my children are so clear. They come out with truths all the time."

Mismatches

I wanted to go to the adult worship service, but it was my turn to teach Sunday school. The minister's meditation was

entitled: "Who Is Caring for Our Children, the TV Set?" I
nabbed one of the parents after the service. "How was it?" I
asked. "It really provoked a lot of discussion today," said
Charlie's father. (There is a time at the end of the service for
the congregation to comment on the meditation.) Charlie's
father summed it up well: "You know, everyone wants intimate families, but we live absentee lives."

It was a misty and blustery day on North Beach. Since the
beach is near the university, there are usually lots of runners and visitors taking in the scenery. Today no one was
around, so I was a bit shocked when a man just seemed to
appear out of nowhere as I came out of the woods. He was
striding along using cross-country ski poles. I guess this guy
is harmless, I thought to myself. Our paths converged; he
smiled and shouted "Hi!" over the crash of breaking waves
on the beach. Yes, he is okay, my instincts told me. "Are you
in training?" I asked, looking down at his poles. He laughed.
"Just trying to build the upper body," he confessed. This
started up our fast pace down the point and back. We covered a lot of ground. I learned that my new acquaintance,
Warren, was a single parent of three children, all under eight
years old. He and his former wife were incompatible as parents. "She wanted us to hire a nanny so we could travel and
make lots of money. Now she is off getting her M.B.A. at
Harvard Business School," Warren said with a hint of bitter-
ness in his voice. "She still thinks *they* are watching." "Who
are 'they'?" I asked. Warren shrugged. "Who knows? My wife
always felt she had to compete with me," he continued, "to
prove herself to the world, I guess." Warren is a tenured professor in economics at the university, but parenting is his
passion. "I was raised on AFDC [Aid to Families with Dependent Children]. My mom was abandoned with four children. She wanted to raise us herself, so she chose to go on
welfare. When my youngest brother was in school, she got a
job and worked her way up to a management position. She

never regretted her decision. I love being a parent. Now I can do it my way—live out in the country and not make the beds. Being a parent is what makes sense of life."

Worth the Sacrifice

Ellen lives in my neighborhood. She is a mother of three children and an endocrinologist, in that order. By choice, she has made her career sacrifices. Ellen knows this is not temporary. Sacrifice, by definition, cannot be made up later. "All of my friends at Yale have made tremendous sacrifices for their children . . . But, you know, I don't have an ounce of regret." I tried to offer some perspective. "This is just one chapter in your life; you'll have time to make your mark." (I meant in medicine.) As I hopped on my bicycle and pushed out of her driveway, she called to me from her front step, "I already have, three times over."

It is not just women who make sacrifices for their families and their children. Once, when I was on the plane to visit my brother in Maine, I sat next to a gentleman who had recently found a new job after four months of unemployment. He was an engineer who had specialized in environmental management. Maine has always been a depressed state, but it was especially hard hit during the recent recession. I congratulated him for getting a comparable job not only in his field but also in his hometown of Portland. "I applied all over the country," he said. "It is not easy starting all over when you are almost sixty." I was lucky. I had a lead when something opened up." I asked about his children. "I could have gone further in my career, but I made the decision long ago to invest the time. They [children] grow like snapping beans. Besides, anything you do in your professional life will probably become obsolete before you die anyway . . . I've never regretted my decision."

An Idol Speaks

There is only one person on the world stage who ever hooked me, woman or man. I would reach for any magazine at the checkout that had her picture on it. I was somewhat embarrassed by this attraction. It felt adolescent—the idol thing. There was the mystique, the grace, the elegance. She was hard to define, a quintessential modern woman but not a feminist. She captivated the world for three decades but wanted no power in it. You had to intuit her; she was not going to tell. She would not be used. Much was written about her but very little said or written by her. Nothing about her life mirrored mine. So where was the bond?

It wasn't until Jacqueline Kennedy Onassis died that I knew. In her eulogy, her brother-in-law, Edward Kennedy, quoted her as having said, "If you bungle raising your children, nothing else much matters in life."[3] A naked statement for such a mysterious woman. Very democratic. It was her only clearly stated value that leaked out into the world, and I have a feeling it was the only one she would have allowed, dead or alive.

Edward Kennedy called Jackie's children, John, Jr. and Caroline, her two miracles. Jackie Onassis had to raise her children as a single parent, under extraordinary circumstances. She did well; she guided her children to adulthood fully intact. It was a miracle for both her and for them.

Given our upside-down world, any child who reaches adulthood, which today means twenty-eight, not eighteen, with a healthy body, mind, and soul, and with a purpose, a direction, a place to belong and with people whom he or she belongs to, is a miracle.

To make our miracles happen, we are going to have to sacrifice any false gods that get in our way. A false god is anything that distracts us from considering children first, not all, but more of the time. A false god can be very seductive. We get pulled in, sucked up, hooked without even knowing it, without really choosing from our deepest values, our highest selves. False gods can even trick us into believing we are doing their bidding in our children's best interests.

Can we make parenting a god, a true god that we make our sacrifice to? Jackie Onassis was called a goddess. She had every *thing* in the world, every conceivable luxury, extraordinary wealth, country and island estates, cruise ships, a treasury of jewels . . . but her testament to the world was about parenting.

Can our children be our miracles? Can we be satisfied with that? Can we let them be our legacy, with no strings attached? Can they be our "mark," without feeling that we must make them into images of ourselves?

How about this for a bumper sticker? "If you bungle raising your children, nothing else much matters in life." Or, for the insider, "Don't bungle it."

4

PRESENCE

PARENTING IS FULL of paradoxes. "Oh, they grow so fast!" parents of grown children tell you with a smile. You stand there with your baby sleeping on your chest in the Snugli®, in the black hole of exhaustion, thinking anesthesia must be a survival tactic of parenthood. As a newborn parent, your time has begun to stretch out, way out to hair thin. You are now acquainted with every hour of the dark side of the clock. You starve for sleep. You count the months left of bending over the changing table and the years left of wrestling with car seats.

Then it happens: your baby is gone. Evaporated. You sort through the baby clothes and cannot quite remember when your child was ever that small. It must be anesthesia. On the eve of her twins turning toddlers, my friend Lynn said,

"I wish we could do an instant replay on that first year. I don't really remember anything; it was all such a blur. It was a rough year, a very hard, tough time. I would never want to go through it again, and yet I am sad. I feel a loss. I wish I could have just enjoyed them more, been more present."

When our children are babies, we do not hold them in the memory of our minds. It was not in the mind that the parent and child made their bond. It was in the body. That is where the memory lies. The holding, the carrying, the snuggling, the rocking, the walking. Once our children leave our arms, we cannot contain them. Growth and development seem to explode in all directions. We stop recording their firsts, their new words; there is just too much to keep track of. In "children's" time, a year passes in a season. It isn't long before you sigh, to the next newborn parent you know, "Oh, they grow so fast." When you hear yourself say that, parenting becomes less physical and more a matter of presence—another paradox in parenting.

What our children most want and need from us is our presence, yet the demands of being a responsible parent put us in direct conflict with being present with our children. As a friend of mine, the mother of three, once said, "Parents are either occupied or preoccupied." One of the greatest challenges in parenting is to keep your children in front of your forehead while you are making a life for them to live in.

The time we have with our children is constantly broken by distractions of every kind. It is always, "Wait a minute," "Later," "Hold on," "I can't right now." When I was a guest on a radio talk show, a frustrated mother called in and said, "I cannot seem to get out from under my house to just be with my child . . . Here I left my outside job to be with her, and there is always something that interferes."

Teachers, too, feel the frustration of distraction when working with their students. Once when I was working in my son's class, his teacher asked me in apologetic tones to straighten up and wash off the shelves. The principal had asked all the teachers to spruce up their classrooms for open house. "This really interferes with the curriculum!" said my son's teacher. "Parents are in the school all the time; they know what it looks like."

One morning, when I was anxiously awaiting a business phone call, my daughter and I were immersed in a pile of picture books fresh from the library. I forgot all about the call. My daughter and I were seated hip to hip, cocooned on the couch, reading down the stack of books. Jolt. The phone rang. It sounded much louder than usual. My daughter did not move; her little body, snuggled next to mine, stiffened. I hesitated too. When I shifted forward to get off the couch, I felt an ache—not from stiffened joints, but from the broken focus. Determined to protect her rights, my daughter sprang off the couch and sprinted toward the phone like a child running home after falling off her bike. She intercepted the call. "Heelllooo," she said, in a long and low voice. "Oh." She dangled the phone from her wrist. With a subdued voice and scrunched-up face, she asked me, "Do you *want* to answer this?" I reluctantly took the phone from her hand. Any ambition I had felt in anticipation of the call drained out of me. I did not want to talk anymore. Worst of all, it was not even the call I expected. The best I could do was to lift her up in my other arm and let her rest her head on my shoulder as I talked.

There are nights when I lie in bed reviewing the day and am stunned that I did not look into my children's eyes, not once during the day. There had been a lot of talking, getting in and out of cars, going here and going there, but there had not been one focused moment. I certainly looked *at* my children, but not *into* them. I was not present. So I get out from under the warm covers and go into their bedrooms and kiss their eyelids.

Not all distractions are unwelcome. Sometimes we are silently gleeful when a friend calls to invite us to a game of tennis or just out for a walk. I question my sanity at times, when I look forward to teaching evening classes even when I'm dog tired. I am off bedtime duty! My husband, who used to be allergic to home maintenance, now lunges for the laundry and insists on going grocery shopping. He has learned the most acceptable way of getting out from under the constant demands of attention from his children. I know there are times when he hides his glee at leaving extra early in the morning, before the scramble to start the day begins.

A Parent's Presence

I used to think that presence was total attention, a clear mind, an absolute focus. For the scattered and distracted parent, I have decided this is not possible. Only people like the Dalai Lama have that kind of presence; at the very least one would have to be child-free. But a parent has a very powerful presence, a different kind of presence.

I was lucky as a child. My parents' livelihoods did not separate us. My father practiced veterinary medicine, and my mother practiced homemaking, along with running my father's business. The base of operation was our home; work and family life wound together. Of course, there were disadvantages, but I never had to experience an absentee father or mother. Before I was of school age, my father took me on calls to the farms where he treated animals. In today's terms, it was on-site child care. If the farm had a bull, I would not go in. But most of the time, I went in as his "assistant." When "on call," my dad was "Doc." My father knew his way around all the farms and could always locate the cow that was sick. I could not tell one cow from another. When he put down his doctor's bag, the cow, with wide and wild-looking eyes, would swing her neck around for a look at my dad. He would cup his hand under her nose. Then, in parent-to-child tones, he calmed her. He held her trust by stroking her head and on down her back. Sometimes it took just a second before the cow seemed to recognize and almost welcome him; other times, it took much longer. I saw my dad treat each animal with great respect and care before he treated them with veterinary medicine. It was a *kything* between man and animal.

Kything is a kind of spirit-to-spirit presence or deep resonance with another. "It is to show yourself, to appear in your own guise, without a disguise or mask."[1] Kythe has the same root word as *kith* or *kin*. Kything is the way your kin know you. Many people believe that both animals and young children can sense out a person: that animals can smell who you really are, and children can either "see" or sixth sense who you are.

I believe parents and children kythe all the time. When parent and child separate for the day, the hugs, kisses, and words of blessing are a kind of kythe: "Good luck on the spelling test." "Have a good soccer game." "Wear your jacket outside." "Drink your milk at lunch." On the surface, these comments seem nothing more than reminders or coaching, but they are actually one way we stay tuned to our children's lives. At exactly 9:30 a.m., we suddenly look at the clock and think, "Christopher is having his spelling test now." Also, our children want to know where we will be and what we will be doing during the day. They keep us in line too: "Don't forget I've got practice tonight."

Any parent who has had a very sick child knows about kything. Instinctively we just want to be with our children at such times. Intuitively we know that our presence helps them heal. If we are not physically present, we are with them constantly in our minds. Or, if your child is performing on stage or on the playing field, you feel the butterflies, you send your child your confidence, your calm if you can. Suppose your son is short for his age and is being teased on the bus by older boys who call him "Shrimp." You talk at home about how he might handle it. Your son wants to take growth hormones. You recommend sitting in the front of the bus near the driver or wearing earplugs. When your son dismisses your "stupid" ideas, you give him a photo of some obscure NFL tackle and say, "Next time the boys bother you, pull out this photo and tell them 'This is my dad.' "

Sometimes a parent's presence is absolutely necessary; no one else will do. I remember when I was in the hospital as a child, I awoke in the middle of the night with a very high fever. I was very agitated and scared. I was probably hallucinating. I wanted my father. In those days, hospitals did not accommodate parents staying with their children. So my father was sleeping on the couch in the lounge down the hall. The nurses tried to protect him: "Your father is sleeping; he is very tired and needs to rest. We can give you something for your fever; you will be fine. Now try to rest." Something in me was going out of control. I was frightened. I would settle for nothing less than my father. Finally, the nurses gave in and went to get him. After all, he was "on call" for me. When he came to my bedside, he did not question me. He just stood by my bed and stroked my brow, just as I had seen him do so many times before when he was treating animals. He kythed with me for the rest of the night. He gave me his sleep.

A parent's presence is no less important during adolescence. Sandy Queen, parent educator, author, and humorist, believes that teenage sex is not so much about coitus as it is about closeness. Adolescents continue to need parental physical affection. At a workshop, I heard Ms. Queen describe a scene with her adolescent son, who comes into the kitchen as she puts a meal together. He stands there with his hands in his pockets, looking down at the floor. He leans against the counter. "That," she said, "is how an adolescent asks for a hug." If the parent asks, "Is there something on your mind?" or "Do you want anything?" the answer is always no. If he doesn't get a hug within a minute or so, he just leaves, hungry.[2]

Adolescents charge through the door at the end of the day and yell, "Mom, Dad!" You yell back, "Yeah!" Your adolescent child never appears. You yell again, "I'm here, upstairs." No answer. You try a third time, "What is it?" Nothing. They just came to touch base and are off again.

Mary Sheedy Kurcinka, author of *Raising Your Spirited Child*, said that adolescents will ask for our attention. Once. "Will you come watch me snowboard?" "Will you shoot some baskets with me?" If we do not come on the first call, they may not ask again. They may *never* ask again.[3]

David Elkind believes that as a society we miss the boat on the adolescent years. We relinquish our care and attention to the adolescent in the name of the child's independence, at just the time he or she most needs our guiding presence. Adolescents need to be hooked into organized activity; they need adult supervision, leadership, role models, and mentors.[4]

When I was first starting out as a parent, I asked our pediatrician, father of three grown children, "What periods in childhood do children *most* need their parents?" "Well, let's see," he considered, leaning back in his chair and rubbing his chin. "Infancy, latency is certainly underrated, and adolescence," he said. "Oh," I said, "that doesn't leave much else, does it?"

A parent's presence is important even beyond adolescence. This summer a young couple attracted my attention when I was taking in the scenery out on the Point. They were lying on a blanket in the shade of an oak, out of the way of bikers and runners. The young man had his arms folded behind his neck; the heel of one shoe balanced on the toe of the other. He was looking up at the sky as he listened to the young woman next to him. She was lying on her side facing him. She rested her head in the hand of her propped-up arm. I sensed they were not lovers. But their familiarity suggested they were more than just friends. The young woman talked at quite a clip. The young man nodded, muttered some "ahas," and broke in for some words now and then. I strained to hear. Amongst their muffled words, I caught their bond. They spoke of their mom and dad. This was sibling talk, big brother counseling younger sister. As the young woman chattered away, she became more and more animated, as if getting closer to an answer. Suddenly she sat up—she had it! "I don't need a therapist, I need my mother!" I heard her loud and clear.

Presence as Vocation

Presence is a powerful component of many professions. Occupational therapists have something called the "therapeutic use of self," the awareness and phenomenon of the healing power of a therapist by presence alone, beyond any therapeutic technique or intervention with the patient. All people who work in close contact with others can use this power of presence.

Physicians can have a strong healing presence with their patients when there is trust and strong rapport. My internist, years ago, used to pour on the reassurance when I came to him several times suffering from terrible flus. "You will get better," he said as he looked at me intently, waiting for his reassurance to sink in, "in five days . . . Don't get discouraged if it takes up to two weeks to be back to full force," he advised. I always felt much better after leaving appointments.

Connie, the director of campus ministry, was fretting one day about what she could, should, or would say at a politically sensitive rally on campus. "If nothing else," I said, "your presence alone will make a statement. Your presence will remind others of the moral issues at hand." "Gee, I never thought of that," she said. This was an entirely new role concept for my outspoken friend, who is used to playing with fire and thrives on high visibility and risk.

Then there is Rosie, who has been the crossing guard at my son's school for thirty years. When she's not standing in the center of the road with her stop sign, she sits in her folding chair on the sidewalk during school hours. She is a kind of guardian angel. When cars are going by the school too fast, it is her presence alone that reminds them to slow down. I know she has slowed me down more than once without moving from her chair or lifting a hand.

A parent's presence should never be underestimated. It is perhaps the most powerful component of parenting. Those children who do best in school are those whose parents have a presence in the schools. Every child thrills at their parents' presence at the baseball, soccer, and basketball games, recitals, swim meets, concerts, Scout meetings, open houses at school, skits, and plays. It is just the more grown-up version of the toddler's incessant "Mommy, Daddy, watch me, watch me!" It is the support and the attention, yes. And it is living a shared life, the ups, the downs, the ins, the outs, the comings and goings, the backs and forths. A parent's presence is like always being backed up so you never have to feel less than whole.

5

RUSH AND RUIN

THERE ARE TWO major times of the day. Before children, these times were called morning and night. After children, they become rush and ruin. How we approach these times sets us up for what happens in between.

Rush

Morning and evening are the most idiosyncratic times of the day for our family. I do best when I rise early, before the rest of the family, and have the time to think through the day, put away any "leftover" yesterday, and do one act of joy, one extra that I will not have time for once the day begins. When the family gets up, I have to be in gear. It always seems that between 7:00 and 7:45 I am half-breakfasted, half-dressed, half-groomed, with one contact lens in. Then between 7:45 and 8:00 a.m., the two halves of my eating, dressing, and grooming come together. That is how a mother's life goes.

My husband is a case in contrast. His rush is very systematic. Get up, into bathroom, into closet, downstairs to breakfast, upstairs for final floss, gather the newspaper, and out the door. I know the pattern well. I shadow him so we can do business.

My son wakes up talking. He doesn't shadow anyone; he just shouts. There is nothing systematic about his dressing. It just happens, all at once. Then on to more important stuff, like the sports page.

My daughter drowses in bed and arises slowly. She staggers to the bathroom rubbing her eyes and always needs lots of hugging and holding before she is ready to take on the day. She spends lots of time in front of her dresser making the apparel choice of the day. Then into the bathroom for primping. She always starts the day with herself.

Just like hair days, we have good rush days and bad rush days. A good rush day is when you are eager. There is something waiting for you in the day and you want to rush to meet it. Everyone in the family has made contact with each other. Our lives get synchronized not just by time but by touch. Hugs, holds, love pats, straightening, squeezzzzzing . . . We need to get a storehouse for the day so we leave feeling full, we do not leave wanting. Everyone's life gets a massage. Angela is having a favorite friend over to play. Toby has a soccer game. Dick will call us when he gets to Seattle, and Linda writes on. Life is a rush, it feels full, it gives us a buzz, we feel *on*. We feel ready.

On the bad rush days, the countertops are cluttered and so is my head. I cannot find the keys to my husband's car that I borrowed yesterday. Nobody wants what there is for breakfast, and Toby digs for his jeans at the bottom of the laundry basket full of clothes that are folded no more and all over the floor. The day is coming undone just like the laundry. The food that I popped in my mouth is not digesting; it is churning. Angela cries because I cannot braid her hair and make peanut-butter sandwiches at the same time. Dick is late. We still cannot find the keys. No one really connects. The words we speak never really register with anyone else. Our lives run on different lines. We begin our day feeling like we forgot to brush our teeth.

A run of good days is exhilarating. A run of bad days can be devastating. The usual course is a mix of more good than bad. It just seems to be happenstance.

Then there is the more deliberate approach:

It was Anne's turn to have the meeting. We talked in hushed tones. Anne's husband was putting their children to bed. The whole house seemed to be bedding down. There was nothing left out. The day had been put away. The energy had settled, and the quiet encircled our small group. When we went into the kitchen to get some tea, I was surprised to see the table set for breakfast. Ann explained that her family sets the table the night before because it helps cut down on the rush in the morning. "How ideal," I thought with a touch of sarcasm. "I'm lucky if my table is clear from the night before."

During bitter cold days this past winter, I drove my son to school. We had discovered that the bus caused an artificial rush. Get out to the bus stop forty minutes before school starts, and ride thirty minutes for a distance of one and one-half miles. I could get there in five. So we skipped the bus. We didn't set the table at night, but we did extend our mornings by half an hour, and many more breakfasts were eaten.

We are a rushing culture. When we rush, we feel a rush. It gets the adrenaline going; we get a buzz. Rushing is our caffeine. It is our drug. We think that rushing proves that we are really living, doing important things, we have a life. Everyone goes around saying, "Oh, I'm so busy." "It's just been crazy." We never dare let there be space, just breathing room. So we do the same to our children: we fill up all their space; we rush them here and rush them there. Soccer, swim team, baseball, ballet . . .

Ruin

Ruin is when the day just ends. Dinner has been a chaotic scene, and the children just get undressed and plop into bed. The whole family is overtired. Somewhere in the afternoon the flow of the day was lost, and the water became very choppy. Ruin is when unresolved issues or conflicts surface and no one can deal with them constructively. Someone ends up crying. Ruin is when we just go to bed without putting the day away, straightening out our house, our minds, and our relationships. Ruin shades the entire day, overcasting it in gray.

Nesting

Most nights, we close out the day in a very deliberate way. Night is our nesting time. My husband and I reserve our evenings as sacred time for family. Our work in the world is done. Night meetings are out. During supper, we unplug the phone. We try to eat together, at the same time and at the same table. We divide up the air time so everyone gets a turn to talk. We share the highlights and the silly tidbits of our day. We laugh a lot because we are all tired and more seems funny.

Nighttime is the one time of the day that our children can count on absolute, undivided attention from one of us. My husband and I each take one child. We usually read a story, but sometimes we watch a special TV program, look at family photos, color while propped in bed, or rub our child's back.

Having one child all to myself, to shower my undivided attention on just him or just her, is heavenly. There is an intimacy that does not happen any other time of the day. I brush her hair. I stroke his brow. We snuggle. I let them soak me up.

Feeding the Soul

After we have rebonded and my children drift to sleep, it is time to feed my soul, to listen to the silent murmurings of the spirit, a time to return to the self. First, I feel great relief that my children are finally asleep; I am released from their clutches. When I bend over their beds to put the last kiss on their eyelids, I marvel at the tender beauty of their sleeping beings; they always seem to return to infancy in their sleep. I look back over my shoulder at the miracle of creation that is my child. If I have the energy, I tidy their rooms and straighten their bed covers. I believe it makes for a more peaceful sleep. It is my final act of parenting for the day. It is my final touch.

Then I retire to my room to feed my soul. I may get a few lines down in my journal, read, take a shower, or just lie on the bed and stare at the wall. This is my time to let go of the day, to release myself from any musts, shoulds, even wants. I let my voice mail answer the phone; I let the doorbell go unanswered. I do not start into work of another kind. Night is on reserve. It is the time to rendezvous with spirit.

The Power of the Night

It is my children who have acquainted me with the night. Not the "all-nighters" of typing term papers or cramming for exams, driving across country, or even of a love affair, but the night of the spirit. Before I had children, I never really knew the night. It was simply the absence of day, the absence of light. But a child teaches you about the spirit of night, the mystery of night, even the power of night. You learn to trust the darkness, to live in it, to welcome it, and even to relish it. Your child teaches you to wake in it, walk in it, rock in it. It is the place that the Phantom of the Opera sings about in the song "The Music of the Night:" "Darkness stirs and wakes imagination / Silently the senses abandon their defenses / Slowly, gently night unfurls its splendor / Grasp it, sense it, tremulous and tender . . . "[1]

It is in the darkness that our world expands beyond the boundaries made by the light. In the day, we live in the world of form and definition. At night, the world has no form. The defining quality is gone. At night, we are free of conformity, culture, custom.

Secrets of the Night

I know a mother who whispers healing messages into her children's ears at night when they are ill to support and speed healing. A friend and teacher told me that before going to bed, she asks her dreams to give her guidance with a student who is struggling. A friend who has lost her dearest friend to cancer speaks to her in the language of the night. It is in the darkness of night that my husband and I can drop our defenses so we can resolve a major difference.

I have come to realize that the way we end or put down the day, the way we straighten up our house to straighten out our lives, the degree to which we digest our experience, and the peace we make with each day, have a great impact on the depth of our sleep and quality of our rest. It is at night that we unwrap the gift(s) of the day and give our sorrows a decent burial. Ending the day whole makes it holy.

I once read about a mother who preserved bedtime as hallowed ground in her relationship with her daughter. No matter what happened during the day, no matter what tension, conflicts, squabbles, or fights she and her daughter had during the day, it was at bedtime that she and her daughter reconnected. It was a time for safety, forgiveness, boundless love, and security. It is like shaking hands on the field no matter what happened during the game.

When bedtime with our children is like handshaking on the field, it becomes a ritual, it is sanctified, it is easy, you can always return to it; you don't have to discuss it, plan it, or make it. And you don't feel quite right without it, like brushing your teeth.

6

FINISHING

THERE IS NOTHING more frustrating than not finishing. Parenting is full of interruptions. A parent can follow his or her own trail of half-finished projects. In parenting, even our interruptions get interrupted: your child bangs her head on the corner of the table, the phone rings, you finally run to answer, and bzzz, they've hung up. We all keep lists in our heads of things we are going to do when the kids get older: put in a perennial garden, redecorate the bedroom, assemble a family album, start a business, read the Sunday *New York Times*, bike across France.

Partially completed projects fill our lives but do not fulfill us. The lack of closure makes us irritable and distracted. It is like the waiter who swept away our favorite dish of fresh grilled salmon with curry sauce before we were finished. It is like getting showered down in the locker room just to find out that the lifeguard has called all swimmers out of the pool because of a sudden thundershower. We always seem to be in the prep stage.

Life makes it hard for our children to finish anything either. How many times have we heard the protest, "I'm not finished!" from our children when we want them to hurry, come, go, or stop as we run out the door. No wonder adolescents lock themselves in their bedrooms; it is the only way they can finish their fantasies. In school, children have their work constantly interrupted by the schedule every half hour. Gym, music, art, library, lavatory break, snack, recess, lunch, the loudspeaker, the fire drill, someone grabs your pencil, Joey vomits, or the class gerbil gets loose. And we wonder why our children are distractible and short on attention.

I had an art teacher once who said, "Successful people are the ones who finish what they start." Her words loomed over me as I frantically tried to finish a weaving project that I had started for the art show. At the time, I thought she was reciting an S.L.E.W. (statement of life experience and wisdom) like "A bird in the hand is worth two in the bush." A quarter of a century later, I had learned to value the weight of her words.

When one gets to midlife, the conservation of energy is of prime interest. Our batteries more often than not seem low. When we do not have closure with the laundry of our lives, our energy dissipates. The cover is off the blender, and our energy gets splattered all over the wall. The momentum is gone. It feels like a bad dream. We move as fast as we can but are always behind. We never catch up.

The Creative Cycle

Energy can be recycled if we finish the whole lap, complete the cycle, or close the circle. It is the interrupted cycle that makes us feel like our engine has stalled on us. Living the life of interruption feels like never getting any exercise. Unless we complete the cycle(s) we began, we will always feel weary because we never get a chance to garner and use the energy generated by completion.

Robert Fritz, author of *The Path of Least Resistance* and *Creating,* says, "When you move though all the phases of the creative cycle [germination, assimilation, completion], you build momentum toward your next creation."[1] The creative cycle can be applied to all levels of creating. Let's use a simple example.

Germination

Family photos sit in the dresser, disorganized and unused. Julie wants to put them together into a family album for all to enjoy.

Assimilation

Julie looks through all the pictures. She gets an idea for how to organize them by season and theme. "As you create what you want to create, each result you accomplish supports the next one," says Fritz.[2] She now knows what size album she needs. She decides to give it to her family for a surprise Valentine's gift.

Completion

She manages her schedule so she can finish on time. "Each time you complete an act of creation, you focus a life force . . . in the stage of completion, your being is ready for another act of creation."[3]

Julie's creation is a big hit with her family. The completion of the project generates energy and launches Julie into another creation, an aquarium for the family room.

Getting Closure

While we were on the beach last summer, a friend and mother of two young children said to me, "I need closure in my life. Since becoming a parent, it has come to the forefront of my needs . . . I need to finish; it doesn't really matter what, just finish . . . making the bed, eating my dinner, putting on my makeup, anything! The best part about being on vacation is not needing to finish. You get closure when the sun goes down."

In one of my parenting classes, a mother of a two-year-old said she never cleans her whole house anymore. "My husband and I used to spend two hours every Saturday morning cleaning the house top to bottom. Now we clean a toilet, dust the dresser, change a bed, vacuum the living-room rug. This has been a very hard adjustment for me, but I've come to realize it is a matter of breakdown; I either do it this way, or I hire a cleaner." Another busy mother structures her cleaning by the clock. She sets her baking timer for ten minutes and then engages in speed cleaning. She is finished when the timer dings. "Time with my kids is precious. My house gets ten minutes a room, my kids get the rest."

Parenting is never finished. You are always "in process" with your kids. But we need to create benchmarks for ourselves and maybe even throw in a ritual to acknowledge our completions in stages. In the language of creating, Robert Fritz calls it the *symbolic gesture*: giving away or selling the baby furniture and maternity clothes, going to our child's preschool graduation, setting up a college savings account, or bringing out the china and putting away the plastic.

Completion Is Critical

In addition to giving us back energy to help launch us into our next project or creation, completion is closing a chapter or phase of our lives so we are released or free to begin a new one. When we do not finish, bring things to an end, close down the chapter, our life can get messy, frustrating, and full of conflict and even loss.

Maureen is a vibrant woman with a magnetic personality and an intellect to match. She raised two well-adjusted, bright, self-confident sons. While they were in elementary school, she attended graduate school. "It worked beautifully. I was always there when they were home. In the evening, they had their dad when I had to be at class or at the library." After she graduated, she landed her dream job. Because it was a leadership position, she put in long work weeks. At that same time, she unexpectedly became pregnant and had a third child. Maureen was in conflict. By then her other children were in junior high and high school. Maureen was finished with "being there" for young children. She had already made her sacrifice to parenting. Her professional life and the life of her family had moved into another phase, another rhythm. Her energy was into her career. She would have to raise this child very differently from her first two. Her husband had been promoted and was traveling on business up to three or four days a week. To top things off, the temperament of her third child was much more difficult than those of her first two children. It was too much. What might have worked beautifully, ended. Maureen had to leave her job, the fulfillment of a long-awaited goal, and start over.

When I was pregnant with my second, my friend Liz gave me some advice. "Decide while you are still pregnant whether this child will be your last." Here is the essence of what she said: "You must know that this is the last time you will be swollen with new life, the last time to feel the baby's turns, kicks, and hiccups in utero, the last time to dream of the unborn child, the last time that you will labor, sweat, grunt, and groan to bring new life into the world, the last time you will hold a newborn in your arms and be the first to say 'Welcome to the world; bless you, my darling.' You must know this is your last, or you may have another, not because your life can hold another child, or you can give yourself to another child, or you even want another child—but just because you haven't finished."

The Last Twenty Degrees

Finishing is not just about conserving energy or completing the creative cycle or keeping conflict and complexity within tolerable limits. There is a spiritual quality to finishing, closures, and endings. Finishing sanctifies our work. Endings are a time of honoring, celebrating, dignifying, releasing, and receiving. Finishing is whole-making.

It has taken me half my life to realize that I am not very good at finishing. I never put much value on finishing. I always finished my work and responsibilities at 340 out of the full 360 degrees of the creative cycle. Then I just dropped the last 20 degrees, the piece left for celebration. I just let them go. For instance, I did not go on my senior trip in high school. The class was going to New York City, and I had already been there numerous times. Mistake. What I did not understand was the deeper purpose of the trip. It was not about sightseeing alone. It was a kind of rite of passage into adulthood, taking responsibility for oneself and each other in a large city, saying good-bye to classmates I had lived with over the last twelve years, and celebrating the ending of a chapter of our lives.

In graduate school, I chose not to attend graduation because I had already paid enough tuition and fees, and now they wanted one hundred dollars more for a cap and gown! Mistake. Some of my fellow students thought I didn't graduate. My thesis was not listed on the program. I did not have a chance to say good-bye to revered faculty members and classmates, and my family (husband at the time) was not honored for his sacrifices and support during the graduate school years. I had denied myself the joy, the acknowledgment, the celebration, and the release of two years of intense work. It left me feeling very unfinished, incomplete, unwhole.

Good-byes

We are much better at celebrating our beginnings than our endings. We feel more comfortable with hellos and greetings than with good-byes and endings.

My mother comes from afar to visit us about three times a year. I noticed that my son never wanted to go to the airport to see her off. On the morning of her departure, he acted as if she had already left. He did not want any good-bye hugs, either.

At first, his behavior irritated me. I felt it was insensitive and rude. I felt like saying, "This is all the thanks you can give your grandmother, who showers you with special attention?" It was not rudeness. He was protecting his feelings. Separation was always tough for him; it gave him a tummyache.

Then one day he had to go to the airport to see his father off to Washington, D.C., for five days. Finally, after the twenty-sixth hug, he released his daddy through the double doors at the gate. My son ran to the picture window. He pressed his four-year-old, full-fleshed palm into the window, holding contact as his dad turned and waved to him several times. Without taking his eyes off the prop plane that was taking his dad, he asked, while wiping his eyes with his shirt sleeve, "Has this ever happened to me before?"

It is important that we learn to say good-bye, to go the full 360 degrees around, so we are free to move on. My friend Nancy has a graduate school classmate and friend dying of AIDS. He called Nancy from across the country to ask if she would host a reunion for several of their mutual friends from both coasts over Memorial Day weekend. Nancy had her reservations and fears for her three young children. She has a medical background and knew the risks. Her friend would have his private quarters, so she agreed. "This is going to be his good-bye. He wants to do it right," she said. Her friend with AIDS was quite frail but insisted on being active with his friends over the weekend. "We had a great time," reported Nancy. "We laughed a lot and cried a lot."

Once my son accompanied his father to a going-away party for one of my husband's colleagues. My son's comment on returning home was, "That wasn't a party; they just had food." When I checked with my husband, he said, "Toby's right. There was no storytelling, speech-making, or roasting. It was just food. They did give her a gift but without any ceremony. It felt very unfinished."

Releasing is an important part of finishing well. It frees us to begin anew. When our family moved recently and my eight-year-old son would have to change schools for the first time, I asked the to-be principal what would help with the transition. He said, "It is important that he be released from Washington School." "Released? What do you mean?" I asked in surprise. "Either his teacher or the school principal needs to officially release Toby," said the to-be principal. "Let Toby know that leaving is not an act of disloyalty; it is okay to change schools. Let him know he will be missed, and send him off with confidence in his ability to make the change and with their blessings."

Finishing Touches and the Closure Craze

It's the finishing touches that make the difference. All parents need finishing touches in their lives. We need the tangible experience of stepping back and saying, "I did that." Today a good friend of mine, the mother of two toddlers and a preschooler, whooped over the phone, "Guess what I did! Last night I stayed up and cleaned all three of my bathrooms. It felt sooo good!" I understood. It's the closure craze, to finish something, anything. We had a good laugh. I then told her what I had done. I got out the polish and started in on the brass doorknob to my daughter's bedroom. All the other doorknobs in my house were badly tarnished. I polished that doorknob until the cloth rubbed clean. It took a good twenty minutes of real elbow grease, and boy, did it feel good. I love to walk by her room and just look at it. My friend laughed and said, "Well, next time I'm over to your house, I won't bother to ask how you are doing; I'll just look at your doorknobs."

Attacks of the closure craze occur in all rhythms of time, by season, monthly, weekly, and daily. During these attacks I have planted petunia beds at night under floodlights, had a No Sale Garage Sale ("No cash, No junk, No kidding" read the ad—I just wanted closure on unused clutter in my house), and stayed up all night reading *Forbidden Fruit,* by Anne Murphy. This was a story that could not be interrupted.

If parents don't get their quota of closures, it is a setup for resentment and third-degree burnout. All parents need to carve out some area in their lives where they feel they have some control, the freedom and time to finish what they start. Some use their professional work as their area of control; others use exercise, Mom's morning out, continuing education, gardening, cleaning toilets, or polishing doorknobs—whatever satisfies the closure craze.

Before we became parents, we were in the habit of doing things start to finish, the whole thing. When we become parents, that does not work anymore. We need to restructure how we do things, usually three at a time. We need to break things down into bite-sized pieces. We need to get closure in ten minutes rather than ten hours or ten days.

When I was in graduate school, I learned to speed-read out of necessity. A book a day. Go for the meat, the essence, jump around, see the framework, get the outline. Since becoming a parent, if I ever waited for the time to read, I would never have a book in my hands. I have to speed-read or not read. I carry books in my purse, in my car; they are stacked on the floor by my bed. Books have a place in my kitchen and in the bathroom. Too bad you can't read in the shower.

Satisfy the closure craze on things that you do well, where you have developed some skill and finesse. Go for immediate gratification. I once dated a man named Greg, who was a fabulous gourmet cook. His culinary presentation was gorgeous. He was working on his dissertation in economics. He needed a diversion, something completely different from crunching numbers, making charts and graphs, and technical writing. "So I started cooking, and I love it," Greg explained. "I use all fresh produce. The handling of the food, the sensual experience, the smells, the taste—it was so totally removed from my work. Cooking refreshed my mind. It was a great relief; I guess it was almost therapy. I always said that it was my wok that got me my Ph.D."

During the final stretch of completing this book, the closure craze hit me hard. I took my children to back-to-back gingerbread house making classes. By the second round, I was drooling, not over the candy but over the project itself. My son was ecstatic. What kid doesn't just love to build with candy? "Mom, I have a feeling this is going to be the best December yet!" Toby said. I kept my hands off his project but was desperate for one of my own. I noticed that the setup next to me on the table was going unused. After the class got under way, I asked the instructor if I could build my own gingerbread house with the unused set. She said, "I really need to hold it in case the registrant comes." My face heated from embarrassment. I sat back in resignation. Halfway through the class, the instructor returned to me and whispered, "I guess it would be okay to go ahead; it looks like a no-show." At first I hesitated. I started in slowly, hoping the other mothers would not see. Once I got into the creative mode and lost my self-consciousness, I let it rip. The instructor noticed my glee. During her rounds, she said,

"Good job, Linda," as if speaking to a child. I giggled. When my husband came to pick us up, I shoved my gingerbread house in his face. "Look what I made!" It was abandoned joy, utter euphoria. A couple of days later, I saw one of the mothers from the gingerbread class. "Well," she said, "what did you do with *two* gingerbread houses?" "Three," I corrected her. "Oh?" she wondered. "I made one!" I said. She looked surprised. "It was a bad case of delayed gratification," I explained. "You know, the closure craze."

7

RESURGE

Energy Talk

"YOU CAN BURN out on parenting too, you know."
Carolyn wanted to make sure that parenting was included
in our discussion of "burnout," that eighties buzzword for
loss of appetite and energy for one's work. This mother and
social worker had set up a painting corner in her living area
as a statement and reminder. Yes, she is a mother and a social worker—and she is also an artist. When people came to
her home, they would often comment, "Oh, Carolyn, I didn't
know that you paint." Her corner was also a reminder to get
to it and do it. Clarissa Pinkola Estes, author of *Women Who
Run with the Wolves*, observes that women do not have
problems doing their art; they just have trouble getting to it.
They always have an excuse—the house, the job, the children, the meals, the phone, the dog, the yard. Carolyn's cor-

ner is her place to create. She knows she must. It is no longer an option, an elective; it has become a necessity. It is her resurge.

No one can be a perpetual parent. There are times when we have to STOP. Parenting on empty can only work in response to the most basic needs. Moody moms and grouchy dads are at risk for developing adult colic. The regenerative diet of a parent is highly caloric. Regular feedings are required. Yet the reality of our lives is that the ways we maintained our energy before children are now gone, or it takes a monumental amount of arranging to just get to our resurges.

In a parenting course I teach, one of the insights that parents find most valuable is about the use of energy. We talk about how much energy it takes to be a growing child, and how much energy it takes to be an evolving parent, and we talk about how hard it is to be either when we're operating on low energy.

One distinguishing feature of parenting today is that there is no room for the unexpected, for upset, for crisis. We are just packed in too tight. One school morning, when our family was preparing to sell our home, I was trying to do in fifteen minutes what needed at least an hour: homework papers lost in the shuffle of papers strewn all over the counter from realtors and contractors, breakfast dishes on the table, phone calls to return, school lunches to make, shoes to tie. Everything seemed to yell, "Do me, do me!" I was running in circles.

My son took the loose energy in the air and played with it. "I feel good . . . da, na, da, na, na, na, na!!!" Next chorus just like the first, "I feeeel good, da, na, da, na, na, na, na!!!" And again, louder now! "Well, I don't feeeeeel good!" I grumbled to myself. Now that we were in the car, the song blared right in my ear, "I feeeel good, da, na, da . . . "

"Will you please stop singing that!" I shouted. My son looked at me indignantly. Killjoy! "What's the matter with you? I was just singing. God, Mom!"

Either we are tired from outside demands (work, school, community) or we are tired from inside demands (children, home, self). Whether we are low on energy from the outside in or the inside out, it has an effect on our parenting and our children.

Here's my low energy list:

- I do not really listen to my children. I ask them "What?" too often.
- I cannot think of anything to do with them.
- I am distracted by most anything: the phone, newspaper, or mail.
- I let them watch TV even when there is nothing good on.
- I cannot get organized.
- I do not look them in the eye enough.
- I want support; I want someone to take over while I lie on the couch.
- I want my husband.

Here's my children's low energy list:

- They are distracted and cannot focus on anything.
- They lose their budding sense of organization; things are just dropped everywhere.
- They want to watch TV, no matter what is on.
- They whine, fall down in a heap.
- They get wound up, have giggling and laughing fits.
- They try to hang on me.
- They want to know when Daddy is coming home.

The lists check out. Yeah, they are my kids all right.

Same Stressors

We do a similar exercise in my parenting class, called "Stacking the Stress." Each parent lists his child's stressors. They stop writing at the point the child will blow or "lose it," as we say. Then it is the parent's turn. Always, the parents are surprised to see that they share similar stressors with their children, i.e., change, interruption, frustration, not getting what they want, being misunderstood, fatigue, being off schedule or out of routine, a series of transitions, an overload of stimulation, or being pushed beyond their level of tolerance.

The stressors are the same for child and parent, just divided into different-sized packages. For instance, take transitions. An adult can relate to the stress of having guests come and go, out-of-town travel, changing jobs, moving, doing five errands in a row, making fifty phone calls in a day, or going back to work on Monday or after a vacation.

Children have the same experiences with transitions, except in different dosages. They may have a hard time with going to bed, having a friend leave, changing the furniture around, eating someone else's food besides Mom's, Dad's or McDonald's, getting a new baby-sitter, leaving the park, or skipping a nap.

Of course, the amount of energy each of us has to give to our parenting and to our children varies tremendously with our circumstances throughout our tenure as parents, from chapter to chapter, from season to season and day to day. Energy is always at a premium.

Fran Kaplan, a social worker and nurturing program trainer and consultant in Milwaukee, has this to say: "Parents are too exhausted these days. If you run your batteries down, what energy do you have to give to others? There is a lack of energy to give to children . . . if children don't see their parents having energy for each other, for others, for reading books, discussing things, then they don't see normal problem-solving." According to Kaplan, "Nurturing is an antidote for violence."[1]

Flow

Specialists in career development advocate that, when making a career choice, it is important that one work in those areas that capitalize on one's strengths and minimize one's weaknesses. When we work in the area of our strengths, we get energized from our work; we are in "flow." It is organizing to our whole life; it is enlivening.[2]

When we work in an area of our weaknesses, then it depletes us, drains us, makes us sick. We are not all created equal; we each have a gift to exercise. That is the most important part of growing and maturing—to find our gift. Many never find it, through lack of opportunity or insight. I believe we know our gift when we are children, on some level. It is in our dreams, our imaginations, our play and pretending. Then along comes school, and our field narrows to logical and sequential learning. Often our gifts never surface. We make decisions about our lifework from the perspective of other factors: economic opportunity, job market, or security. Yet this never completely satisfies us. If we never find our gift and bring it to life, there is always a restlessness, a gnawing feeling that we are missing something.

As in any work, we need to put our gifts into parenting if we want to be in "flow" more of the time. Otherwise, parenting will be a depleting, draining experience much of the time. Child psychologist David Elkind says parents today think they are supposed to *entertain* their children, to take them to amusement parks, roller rinks, movies, or fast-food restaurants with fancy play equipment. No resurge for the parent there. He advises parents who have limited time to spend it in the strongest possible way—by sharing themselves with their children. That means including our children in things we like or need to do, be it gardening, cooking, or faucet-fixing.[3]

Energy Boosters and Depleters

The best antidote to burnout in parenting is to know your energy boosters and depleters. Know your children's as well. Boosters should be part of your staple diet. Stay away from depleters as much as possible, or at least balance them with boosters.

Name the things that deplete you. Here's my list:

- Shopping of any kind, especially grocery shopping
- Hauling groceries and putting them away
- Cooking under pressure: "Mom, I'm hungry!"
- Piled-up laundry
- Negativity, mine or anyone else's
- Night meetings
- Over-scheduled, back-to-back activities
- Maintenance parenting: "Brush your teeth, eat your vitamins"
- Tired, bored, or hungry children
- Mess, clutter, and chaos
- Amusement "palaces" for children, inside or out
- Unfinished projects
- Worry; restless nights
- A series of phone calls
- Waiting, especially in the pediatrician's office with a sick child

Energy Boosters

Name energy boosters. Here's my list:

- Water: oceans, lakes, waterfalls, creeks, rivers, fountains, showers, baths, pools, beaches, fresh snow, rainfall, sparkling drinking water
- Walking by water, in the woods, or up a mountain
- Being alone with my husband
- Heart-to-heart talks with close friends
- Reading good stories to my children
- Biking with my family
- Swimming with my kids

- Creative projects with children
- Playing strategy games with my children
- Roasting marshmallows on an open fire
- Browsing in a bookstore by myself
- The Farmers' Market
- Flower gardens, especially mine
- Creating of any kind
- Decorating for holidays and season changes
- Reading
- Teaching
- Music, my eclectic collection

Drop, delegate, or reduce your depleters. To get time for your boosters, you may have to build them into your schedule, barter with your spouse, children, or friends, or beg, when you are desperate. I use all three strategies. If we spend all our time and energy on things that deplete us, we will burn out, and even worse, we will not enjoy being a parent. We may even resent our children. As Randall Colton Rolfe, author of *You Can Postpone Anything but Love,* writes, "It is a hard truth that if you aren't enjoying your parenting, your child isn't enjoying being a child."[4] Parenting is a balancing act of energy. To keep our energy up, we must know ourselves well, know what recharges us and fast, and we must know what we can do *with* rather than always *for* our kids.

Deborah Fallows, author of *A Mother's Work,* knew she would not get far in motherhood without exercise, so she built it into her daily schedule. Fallows also found she needed to drop the homebound parenting model, where activity, learning, and play were organized within the home. It worked well for her friends but not for her. "We do much better outdoors. We visit, visit, visit, museums often, the library, hotels to buy a Coke and ride the elevators, pick-your-own-crop farms."[5] Being out in the world with our children has its energy conservation advantages. Children will draw energy from out there rather from their parents' energy batteries.

Doing things with our children that energize us, things that we enjoy, will buoy everyone. Don't be put off if your child's first reaction to an idea is "No!" There seem to be two kinds of kids—the nayers and the yeahers. Some kids will try anything once and may never do it again. Other kids warm up more slowly and just have to do it, once, twice, or more times, before they get hooked. My son insists that he hates biking, yet he reminisces in the wintertime about the places we went on our biking expeditions. In early spring, he is the first one out on his bike, tracking through the slush and cracking up ice under his wheels.

One Way

When joy is around, children will join in on some level, either with both hands and feet, or they will just hang around, wanting to be close by, like parallel play. My hairstylist is a passionate gardener. It is her energy booster, her resurge. She does major gardening planning for her five-acre homestead and has planted five thousand bulbs and a dozen perennial beds. She has two sons, ages nine and eleven. The nine-year-old joins her in the gardens. "He is my little botanist; he notices every new bloom, knows the names of the flowers . . . he likes to putter in the soil; he helps me plant sometimes. On good days he may even do a little weeding." The other son wants nothing to do with gardening. " . . . Absolutely no interest. So I built him a basketball court off the side of the house. He shoots baskets, and I sow the soil. That way he is happy, and I'm happy. He sees the progress of my garden, and I see the progress of his lay-up shot."

Wrong Way

One spring, during school break, I was trying to think of some special things to do to highlight the week, to break us out of winter and into spring. We had lived in Wisconsin for five years and had not yet visited the infamous Milwaukee Zoo that so many people had raved about. What kind of a mother was I, anyway? So my husband and I took the day off from work, and we all went to the zoo. It was a beautiful, sparkling spring day. Everything was fine until we hit the big-city driving, and I went down a one-way street. That extended our car ride and shortened my husband's patience. (His tolerance for car confinement was at its limit before the one-way-wrong-turn.) Once in the zoo, the first place you hit is the pavilion, complete with concession stand. Of course, the aroma hit hard, and our kids were suddenly starving. The puny sandwiches and wholesome fruit I had packed didn't have a chance. My husband had to stand in line for thirty minutes just to give our order. The smell of zoo hung heavy in the air, not particularly appetizing. After lunch, we roamed from animal house to animal house looking at the various creatures through the plate glass. The neurotic behavior of the animals was depressing, like that of the elephant who endlessly swung her trunk from side to side, broken only by swirling motions of her head. My daughter had to be held up so she could see over the railings. She was in no hurry. She wanted to watch the animals eat and groom. She wanted to pet something. My son wanted to race through; he had just studied marine life in school. Finally, he saw the aquatics sign and raced off without us. When my husband found him, the exhibit was closed for repairs. When we reached the exit, we were all cranky and irritable. I felt cheated out of a precious spring day. Of course, my husband and I had a squabble on the way home about heaven only knows what. When we were finally home, my husband happily announced, "Well, that's it for zoos. Off the list."

Another Way

During the same school break we made another choice. We went to Devil's Lake State Park. "How could such a beautiful place have such a name?" I asked my friend. "It's the white man's translation of the Native American word for 'spirit,' " she said. My son wondered what we would do there. So did lots of other people, because the place was deserted. The temperature was forty degrees; we wore our wool hats and winter jackets. We needed boots for the mud. We picnicked behind the bathhouse to protect ourselves from the high winds. The kids ate my puny sandwiches and my orange and apple slices, because I didn't have any competition. It seemed we were the first to comb the beach after winter's deposit of shells, stones, and sticks. We listened to the clinking of ice washing up on the beach, a sound that I had never heard before. We hiked the bluffs that encircled the thawing lake below and talked about the pink sedimentary rock. We saw hawks glide on the wind currents overhead and watched for the eagles that make their homes in the cliffs. We met up with rock rappelers at the top and watched them secure their ropes. The children had filled their lungs with fresh air; the wind had brushed their hair. Their eyes had traversed the majesty and grandeur of a lake guarded by towering sandstone cliffs. When we returned home, we were happy-tired. It was a perfect night for a simple supper like soup and salad, a bath, a book, and bed. It had been an exquisite day. A real resurge.

Part II

====

Growth Spurts

8

UNTAMED LOVE

I STARED AT the card. "Your birthday brings me joy," read the sentiment. It was okay, not exactly one of my better selections. I'm one of those who used to comb the card racks in search of the perfect inscription. I had the best card stores within a twenty-five-mile radius of my home staked out. That was before children. Nowadays I walk around muttering to myself, "I used to be such a thoughtful person." Birthdays of relatives breeze by me now. Forget the "I'm thinking of you" notes and phone calls "to say I care." I sigh and have to forgive myself for another year. Since becoming a mom, it is hard for me to get to my desk, find a stamp, or remember to pick up the "any card is better than none" at the grocery store; or else it is just too late, even for the "I'm sorry I missed your birthday" card. On the surface, the constant distractions of motherhood are my excuse. But maybe there is something else going on.

I gripped a fist of hair, trying to pull just the right words to write in my friend's birthday card out of my head. "Mommy, Mommy, what are you doing?" whined my daughter. She pulled the card over the edge of the table for a better look, bending it in half. Inching the card back on the table, I pleaded with her for a little bit more patience, the amount between the tips of the thumb and index finger. I was getting closer to just signing "Love, Linda." Something had to give. I was trying too hard. I was trying to express the depth of my feeling and appreciation without really revealing the depth of my feeling and gratitude. Tricky? Hard? I did it before. Why could I not do it now? During the days when I had the time, I concealed my love in well-worded verse that spoke for me, instead of from me. I just didn't know any better.

My daughter has her own paper now and scribbles freely on the paper next to me, while my pen does not move. Why do I hesitate so? If I tell my friend how I really feel about her in the birthday card, I'll scare her away. I ran through the possibilities: "I am wild about you; I love you as a sister; you embody love; I love all our times together." Something stops me.

"Mommy, look what I made!" I envy my daughter's fluid work habits. Not waiting for me to respond, she hops off her chair and brings her drawing to me. The paper gets crumpled between us as she lunges at me for a hug. Now I know what is going on. Right before me, I have a love that is wide open, wholehearted, and free, the love between parent and child, untamed love. Using a card as a place to put my love seems like a distant second cousin in comparison.

It is what we remember from childhood that returns to us after we become parents ourselves. We were hugged, carried, cuddled, rocked, hummed and sung to, stroked, swayed, swung, swirled, squeezed, fondled, scooped up, swooped up, piggy-backed, cooed over, wooed over, and showered with kisses. Unrestrained, unbridled, untamed love. It was before we had words to speak and before our parents thought we understood the words they spoke, that we knew the language of love the best. Any excuse is fine, and any time is good: Aha! I found you hug, I'm ready for the day squeeze, keep me safe handhold, isn't it exciting swirl, I want to cozy up cuddle, let me see pick-up.

Hugs were the best. They were the healers. To hug is to hide from the world for a while. To be private with our pain, to smell the protection of our parents, to calm by the slow and regular rhythm of their breathing, to feel total love by total contact, and to heal and be made whole again. After a healing hug, the light is brighter, the colors deeper, the breath fuller.

Once I asked a community leader and mother of four how children had changed her life. She said, "I don't take BS anymore. I don't have time for it." Once you have fallen in untamed love, the tamed "b-lue s-ky" expressions are abandoned. You just can't find the time for tamed love anymore.

A time comes when even the open valve on parent-child untamed love closes in. A neighbor once confided in me that she was in therapy with her son. She wanted to talk, so I asked her about it. "When I go to pick him up at school, he runs for me and jumps up into my arms. It is embarrassing. The other boys make fun of him and call him a mama's boy." I asked what the psychologist thought. "Oh, he says Chris is too emotionally dependent on me; he needs to learn greater independence." Chris is seven years old and in second grade. His mother is a single parent and works as a supervising surgical nurse full-time, and the father is half a country away and sees his son once a year in the summer for two weeks. We are all so anxious about fitting in, being socially accepted. Explicit mother-son love is not okay, even if that's all you've got.

Six years later, and in another part of the country, another mother speaks of mother-son love with a shade of uncertainty. Her son Jeff is thirteen, the same age that Chris would be. Jeff's mother talks about her son as half-child and half-man. She speaks of his fetishes with flick lighters and firecrackers, how he spent lawn-mowing money on a TV for his room, how he loves candles and incense and gets the wax all over his stereo, how he takes off on his bike and doesn't tell her where he is going, how he wants to hang out at the mall, yet how on the most humid days of summer he wants to hang all over his five-foot, one-hundred-pound mother. Jeff's mom explained, "I told him, 'Pleasseee, Jeff, stop hanging on me. I love you too. We can hold hands if you want to.' Of course you can imagine what he said to that: 'Mom, are you weird or something?' " Finishing her story, she turns on the ignition of her Isuzu and shouts out the window, "I guess it is normal." She shrugs her shoulders. "I don't know."

Perhaps more familiar is the picture of the child pulling away first. Several years ago a neighbor warned me, "It's all over at seven; they [sons] don't want to be hugged or kissed by their parents anymore. One day they are on your lap, and the next day they are not—ever again."

It's as much of a struggle to keep untamed love going with fathers and daughters. It's the sex thing. A friend of mine has a daughter who is eleven years old and budding. The family is very close. Time together as a family is sacred. As my friend Katie put it, "We don't have to get a baby-sitter to have a good time." Katie shared with me one day how her husband, Tom, was struggling to find new ways to be intimate with his daughter that would be comfortable for them both. Tom is feeling the tension first. Father and daughter had napped together when she was a young child and even slept together on the nights she was sick or had a bad dream. "I can still stroke her hair and rub her back," sighs Tom. His tone wonders when those might have to go too.

The parent-child combos that do not lose touch really stand out. They catch your eye. One Sunday a father and his two teenage sons sat directly in front of me. The father, somewhere in his forties, was a mesomorph. The muscles of his forearm bulged in front of my face as he gripped his son's opposite shoulder in a firm hold. His son, who looked to be about twelve years old, did not resist and leaned into his dad slightly. The elder son, probably fourteen or fifteen, leaned across his younger brother to whisper something in his dad's ear. Blood ran into their faces as the threesome huddled forward. Flushed, they sat back up and shifted in their seats to squelch an outburst of laughter. The father threw the elder son that parental look that says, "What am I going to do with you?" and smiled at him with tender eyes. The elder son took it! For a moment, I felt love for the dad. It is a real turn-on for a woman-mother to see a man-father nurture his children in his own right, in his own "untamed love" way.

Once when my husband and I were in the midst of our biannual marriage revival, we told each other what we *now* found attractive about the other. (Since parenthood, some of the former shapes and shades of our relationship have changed.) Somewhat to my surprise, and my husband's as well, I started with, "When you are caring for Angela and Toby, being completely yourself, and I am out of the picture, when you substitute their names for the main characters in stories, talk over serious matters in the shower, turn up the stereo and sing and shout, when you dress them in the wildest color combinations and make 'Daddy' toast for them, that is when I absolutely adore you!"

The young child is always ready to unleash his untamed love. Children live for it and on it. It is tops on their list of "things to do." When their gestures of untamed love are rebuffed because someone doesn't have the time, or this isn't the *right* time, or they've gotten too big, they become confused and disoriented. They feel deeply hurt; they are wounded. They withdraw. We do not see their wound because they do not bleed. They do not even cry. They just slowly become tame in their love.

There are some who reach adulthood with their untamed love intact, or else they have learned to reopen the valve. The friends who have stuck with me from young adulthood on into middle age know about untamed love. My life has been a modern one. I moved away from my childhood home, bound for college; five different cities in four different parts of the country followed. Tamed love never survives a move. It's good for about a year and almost vanishes in five. It's not from a lack of interest or feeling. It is just too hard to keep it going. It takes too much effort, too much energy. Untamed love revives quickly with any kind of contact. You don't have to live close to be close. It is often said that a mark of a true friend is the ease in picking up where you left off. I believe it is a shared history of untamed love that makes the "pick-up" phenomenon possible.

My friend Anne and I harmonize in our low- and high-octave laughter. When I call her office, she sends her next appointment down the hall for a cup of coffee so we can snatch some phone time. When I call long distance to Louise, she shrieks on the phone and shouts my name. Louise and I always part by exchanging "I love yous." Mary's face lights up into a smile when we greet one another. She looks into my eyes to see what is going on and then always asks the straight-to-the-heart question. When she sees pain, she hugs me and hums into my chest.

We think untamed love is kid stuff. It is spirit stuff.

Wherever you find untamed love, there will be spirit, and wherever you find spirit, there will be untamed love. I first became conscious of this years ago while attending the weekly worship services of a uniquely ecumenical and close-knit spiritual community.

Every Sunday adults and children reunited after worship and Sunday school on their way to the communion table. The reunion was jubilant and noisy with the assorted love languages of multiple families. Children leapt into parents' arms after searching through the maze of skirts and pants. Parents beamed at their child(ren), and the child(ren) beamed back. Some hid their faces between their parents' legs or in the napes of their necks. The "child-free" and senior members of the community embraced the children in their own way: a broad smile to say "Welcome," or a "Good morning" whisper into their small friend's ear.

The minister began Communion by retelling the story of the Last Supper to the children. "It was a gathering of friends," he explained. "We remember how they shared their lives by eating this bread and drinking this wine." By now several small chins rested on the table. Before the children's eyes, he broke open the round loaf of warm bread. Holding the bread open for the children to smell, he said, in words they could hear but not understand, "We share this bread remembering that our lives are broken open." As he poured the wine from the large vessel into cups to be shared, he said, "We drink from this cup remembering that our lives are poured out like wine."

In the hour that had passed, candles were lighted, hymns sung, prayers said, Scripture read, joys and concerns shared, and a homily delivered. But it was at the table encircled by children, where the bread was opened and wine poured, that untamed love broke out. Warm hand held warm hand like fresh-baked bread, and tears poured down more than one face. Underneath all the brokenness, all the pain and imperfections of life, is a reservoir of untamed love.

Once I happened to see a miniature gift card I had given my father at Christmas several years before. He had saved it in the top drawer of his bureau. It was the same drawer I had rummaged through as a child looking for milk money between socks, handkerchiefs, wallet, and watch. I reached down into the drawer and opened the card. "This is not what I most want to give you ... " It hurt to read it. My father had been in chronic, intractable pain for six years. What I most wanted to give him was a way out of his pain. But the pain could not be pulled out or drugged over. Some time later I broke free into untamed love. Sharing tears, I joined his pain, the grief of lost life, and the fullness of untamed love. Untamed love takes it all; it can break its way through anything.

Some time ago I threw my collection of greeting cards away. They had yellowed. Now I try to keep blank notes on hand for when untamed love breaks out. I do not linger over them now; I don't have the time. I try to get the untamed words onto the paper before I get a tamed thought to stop me. I still can't get to my desk or find a stamp very often.

Today is Rosh Hashanah. I wrote an untamed note to a friend. Our friendship needed healing since our quarrel earlier in the year. It took seven minutes from desk to mailbox. I guess untamed love is all I have time for anymore.

9

PROP UPS

What's a Prop?

CHILDREN LOVE TO work. To work is to play. To play well you need props, good props. A good prop helps you grow; it is the best kind of toy. It must be easily accessible. It can be shared and used in lots of different ways. Props are good for all ages. A prop is often but not always a thing.

Children are always looking for props. They are prop finders and makers. They find them in the kitchen, junk drawer, garage, basement, and closets. With a flashlight you can play Tinkerbell darting around the room or hide-and-seek in the backyard at night. The discarded tire in the garage becomes a trampoline or a swing. Big boxes can be a cave or a nest. A saucepan can be a hat or a guitar. A bubble bath can make a beard or a new hairdo. Toilet paper makes a great pull toy.

Children see props in everything. Their discovery of props forces us to take a different view of things. In the schoolhouse of parent education, we have learned not to scold or punish for their discovery of new functions for old forms. But we still hold onto "everything in its place." When our darling has drawn a picture all over the bathroom mirror with the toothpaste, we have learned to recite the words of reality, saying, "Toothpaste is not for making pictures; it is for cleaning teeth." We have structured without scolding but may have squelched her spirit a bit too. She makes a silent protest. "What do you mean my drawing [inspiration] is a NOT?"

With their discovery and use of props, children prod us to grow, to break out of our usual way of doing and seeing things that has wrapped itself around our beings and set us in dried conformity.

There are two kinds of props that crack our shell the best. These top-of-the-line props come in two varieties: Transformers and Connectors.

Transformers

A Transformer is a kind of prop that is a catalyst for change, not the toy that changes from a spaceship to a robot and back again. A Transformer works by changing something to a higher value, or it can change someone to a higher state of being.

Take water. It can make mud, popsicles, snowballs, bubbles, puddles, waves, and rainbows. You can spray it, freeze it, or heat it. It can be any color you want—just add food coloring.

You can metamorphose a monster kid with it. I know more than one parent who will bubble-up the tub and soak down the kid with a tepid bath. Just dump in some flotation toys, and you've got thirty minutes of peace.

You can even metamorphose a monster Mom with it, as I

learned from a senior friend of seventy years of age. She remembers well an afternoon she was struggling to clean the house for evening guests with three young children underfoot. She was in a sour mood as she scrubbed the floor on her hands and knees. Her four-year-old son decided to put her out of her misery. With garden hose in hand, that he had pulled through the screen door, he pressed the nozzle and proceeded to flood the entire floor. "There, Mom, all done!" her son said proudly. "I didn't know whether to laugh or cry; I think I did both," explained my friend. "I did not yell. Instead, I went to the phone and canceled our dinner date that I had never wanted in the first place. I explained that there had been an accident in the kitchen."

The best props are discovered. That's what Dr. Myrin Borysenko found out while he was in the midst of a major research project at Tufts University. Borysenko came down with a flu-like illness at a critical point in the project. He could not afford any time off. The pressure was mounting, and so was his temperature. Borysenko was desperate. He had to get out of his predicament. So he did the unthinkable. He went to a healer whom he had heard about from his graduate students. When Borysenko found the healer, he was as much surprised by the healer's manner as by his method. Without any introduction, the overweight, TV-watching, tattooed healer-guy handed him a plastic container of a blue solution and nodded toward the bathroom: "Mix this in a half-filled bath and soak for thirty minutes and then go." Borysenko did as he was told. After soaking in blue water for twenty minutes, Borysenko felt so ridiculous that he started laughing. After ten minutes of his laughing treatment, he got out of the bath, dressed, went home, and felt much better. The hard part was explaining to his wife why he was blue below his belt.[1]

When we become parents, we need to get our props in

place and fast! A participant in one of my Mom-Esteem classes told how she coped with trading in a career in management, where she had lots of control, for parenthood, where she felt she had none. After caring for two children under the age of two all day, this mom was in her bear state by late afternoon. As soon as her husband came through the door in the evening, she handed over the kids and went into the basement to hibernate. She did not emerge until she changed back into a human being. What was her secret? Quilting on her sewing machine. "I ran that motor hard," she said. "You could see sparks flying off the needle."

Parents sometimes adopt the props of their children. We get introduced to things we just never thought of before. Once when I was introducing my three-year-old to ice skating at the local rink, I kept myself interested in our snail's pace by watching the trained skaters. I became transfixed by one skater in particular. This skater was not athletic but skated with a seasoned grace and beauty. She had the legs and waistline of a twenty-five-year-old, but in profile I could see that her back was slightly curved. When she skated close to us, I was shocked to see the face of an older woman, fifty-five or so. She shared the love she felt for her sport and herself with a glowing smile.

Later, I talked to her as we all changed from skates to boots. "I bet you started skating very young," I said. "It is wonderful that you are still at it." She smiled as she wiped off her blades. "No, actually I didn't start until my son started taking hockey lessons. He was ten and I was forty. It looked like so much fun I decided to take some lessons myself. I've never stopped. I skate almost every weekday. You know, at the time I started I was overweight and had tried every diet without success. When I started skating, the pounds just dissolved, and weight has never been a problem since." I dared to ask how old she was. "Sixty-two next month," she said without hesitation.

Sometimes a Transformer is simply a matter of attitude. You can bypass the prop and go straight to change. One morning, after an especially busy weekend, my son was wired and operating in overdrive. It was a whiny way to start the day. It was just too much fuss to get ready for school. After my fifth reminder to my son to get his shoes on before the bus came, he called me the "D" word. In his frustration he shouted, "You dork!" I lunged at him, turned him upside down, and paraded around the island in the kitchen. I continued until I heard the sound. It took three times around, and then he started, a full-force eruption of belly laughing.

Transformers work well for all ages. Good timing enhances the power of Transformers, whether the change is behaving or healing.

Connectors

The second top-of-the-line prop is the Connector. These props bring people together, make connections, build community, and strengthen bonds.

One of the best Connectors I know is the ball. It is often baby's first prop and among his first words. This prop is made in many materials and bears such nifty names as Kushi and Nerf. It is even the subject of such positive slang expressions as: "She is really on the ball," "He will get the ball rolling," and, "We had a ball." With ball in hand, fathers feel like real pros when playing with their kids. Now here is a prop dads know how to handle.

One of the best things about a ball is its intergenerational appeal. When my seventy-year-old mother came for a visit from twelve hundred miles away, my son welcomed her with an invitation. As he swung the door open, home from school, he said, "Hi, Grandma Judy! How would you like to play football?" Without waiting for an answer, he gave her a choice: "Touch or tackle?" They were well matched. She knew the rules, and he could run. Thirty minutes later they came back in the house, laughing and reconnected.

Balls have tremendous power; they can assemble more than eighty thousand people into a single stadium and millions more in front of television sets for major-league games. On a smaller scale, balls build community better than organized religion. It is the ball that gets parents connected for car pools, after-game snacks, and phone trees. Parents huddle together to chat and cheer on their favorite team. Any group of parents who have weathered a game in the cold wind and rain feel a special bond. One mom lamented at the end of our soccer season, "I hate to see soccer end; this has become my social life."

Stationed at the center of our cul-de-sac or "circle," as it is affectionately called, is a portable basketball backstop and hoop. A neighbor with two sons donated it, and now it has become the common gathering place for the children, the dads, and, on occasion, the moms on the circle. The kids spend as much time climbing on the base and swinging from the posts as they do shooting baskets. Dads use it for after work cool downs and weekend pickup games. One neighbor complained to the city that this circle centerpiece was an eyesore and a hazard to utility trucks. This threat to community caused a minor revolt among our assertive youths. The city and the complainant backed off.

Books can be powerful Connectors too. Books are just an extension of the breast. After the breast come books. You can start reading at six months. Reading on Dad's lap has all the advantages of breast-feeding, without the sore nipples. It can bond parent and child, calm and comfort, and shift the child into a state of slumber. It can be a time of great intimacy, free of distraction or intrusion. As the inside story is read to the child, the outside story is being created between parent and child. This is Daddy changing his voice to be the big bear or the squeaky mouse. It is wiggling toes with all the rhyming words. It is being the main character, name and all. It is reading a favorite book every night for a month. The story never finishes, it just goes round and round. Parent reads to child, child reads to parent, adult child reads as parent.

Books connect all sorts of people—parent to child, friend to friend, and teacher to student. My friend Jackie is a gifted teacher. She connects easily with children, even ones who are not so easy. Jackie told me of a chance meeting with a woman named Sonya with whom we had both worked briefly fourteen years before. Neither of us had seen her since. Sonya was a "float" in our school. She helped out in the office or classrooms as needed. "You know," Jackie remembered, "Sonya was different. She was kind of impish. I remember a book she read to the kids that at the time I thought was weird. It was a story about a boy who was shrinking. Every time he tried to say something and people didn't listen, he would shrink." "What was the book?" I asked. "Ah, I think it was *The Shrinking of Treehorn*[2]," said Jackie. "You know, that book comes into my mind, almost in a haunting way, every time I'm rushing around the classroom trying to get things done and one of my kids is trying to tell me something and I'm not listening. I remember to stop shrinking and start listening."

Family stories are great props to pull out when you're stuck in an airport, in line, or you are just too tired to focus your eyes for a bedtime story. The ones that stick in our minds are the funny ones, and each time you tell them they get funnier and funnier. Laughing is the way people connect best. Humor is a great adhesive.

One story that always gets a howl in my birth family is the thruway-rest-stop one. We were in for a long haul of thruway driving. We were on summer vacation. It was hot and humid. The windows were rolled down (this was in the days before air conditioning), and the traffic whizzed by. No one tried to compete with the noise, so we rode in silence. We three kids dozed off and on in the back seat, while my parents stared at the road like zombies. My dad pulled off at one of those thruway service centers and told the attendant to "Fill her up." We all just sagged in the heat. As soon as my dad had paid the attendant, he stepped on the gas and we were off! It took almost a mile before anyone noticed. "Hey, where is Mom?!" My father pulled up his cap and looked in astonishment at the empty seat next to him. My mom had stepped out of the car to go to the bathroom back at the rest stop. We took the next NO U TURN.

Let's face it, we never grow out of our need for props. Without a prop, we think we have no access to play. It is our children who open up the field of props to us. Who else gets us on swings, throwing a football, flying a kite, roasting marshmallows, or diving into waves? One of my college professors said, "Successful people not only work hard, they play hard too." This is supported by a 1984 study done by the Center for Research on Women at Wellesley College. The two main components of satisfaction in life for the women they studied were mastery and pleasure.[3]

Parents connect best with their children, and children with their parents, when they have a prop to share, something that will make them connect with one another and grow up a bit or grow a bit more whole. Otherwise, the "thing" would not hold anyone's attention for very long.

A parent is the most highly prized prop in a child's life. It is through our support and attention that he or she can connect with the world and transform-up into maturity. Like all good props, we need to be easily accessible and be used in lots of different ways such as companion, cheerleader, and guide. Chances are, if we have been a good prop, our children will include us as players in their lives.

How Many Props Do You Have?

Survey your garage, basement, and closets. Are they filled with age-segregated toys, or are there some props that all members of the family can use and share?

Are there places/spaces in your home where props are welcomed, where a mess is okay, where one can tinker and experiment, where form has no specific function?

Do you have some open-ended things for your children to play with, such as large cardboard boxes, building blocks, or colorful fabric?

What were your favorite props as a child? In what way(s) or form(s) are they still with you today? Have you shared them with your child yet?

As your child grows older, does the number of props you share with your child increase?

What new things do you want for yourself, for your child? How can they be used as a catalyst for growth, a catalyst for connection?

Postscript: Props Do Not Make Good Presents

Years ago, a friend had to excuse herself from our conversation to run to the hardware store to pick up a present for her son's friend, who was celebrating his ninth birthday. I was curious, so I asked what she was getting for a birthday present at the hardware store. "Oh, a set of pulleys, rope, and some magnets. It probably won't be the most popular gift at the party, but he'll be playing with it the longest." I suspect she was right on both accounts.

Props do not make good presents, especially not from the almighty parent. For my son's seventh birthday, we had to return all the "prop presents" in exchange for real presents—toys. My son came to me a couple of days after his birthday and told me how unhappy he was about his birthday presents, the prop ones. "I can't believe you got that indoor garden kit and that model of a skeleton. Those aren't presents!" he barked. We had already agreed on no books for presents two birthdays before. I had not thought I was in violation of the birthday-present code of ethics. It has nothing to do with use. My son takes twenty-five books out of the library at a time, spends hours working on Legos construction, and has a giant pumpkin patch every year. Still, props hold no present appeal.

A real present has to have instant impact, something plastic and shiny, with decals and a short play life. Something dispensed with in about the amount of time it took for the commercial to run.

Toys mark a child's time in history. Toys are the culture's ethos in hand. The ethos of today is simple: See it, want it, get it, discard it. Toys are prescriptive: One Way and One Age. Toys are the props of the popular culture. They make a child feel "in"-cluded.

Toys have immediate impact; they get the wide-eyed and open-mouthed reaction and spontaneous affection for the parents, the arm hold around the neck. It brings tears to our eyes that such junk brings such joy.

To give some toys on special occasions tells the child that we can suspend our own higher values for the moment, throw valuable money away, be nonutilitarian and frivolous so that our child can experience the "want it-get it" magic. That is where we are headed, but we have a long way to grow.

This issue is not just for the ten-year-old and under; it runs the gamut of the parenting years. On the eve of our college graduation, a friend of mine was down. I suspected it was graduation blues. "No," he said. "It's my parents. They took me out to dinner last night and gave me *this* for a graduation present." In a side-handed manner, Shelby handed me an expensive watch. I held it in silence as he continued. "This is a gift you would give someone leaving the firm after twenty-five years. It's even *engraved*," he said, as if speaking of his tombstone. To Shelby, this was a cold gift even though it was personalized with his name. There was nothing of Shelby in it. The watch was like his relationship with his parents. There was nothing that marked his growth, just time. There was nothing that connected him to his parents, just distance. It was not a prop, it was not a present, it was a NOT. I doubt he ever wore it.

Do you remember what your parents or anyone else gave you for a present on your fifth birthday, eighth, twelfth, fifteenth, or twenty-fifth? Probably not, unless you got a horse. But chances are you do remember if your parents tried to get you what you most truly wanted at least once. Not to spoil you, but so you would grow up believing that you were worthy and capable of having what you most wanted.

A while ago my son said he needed new underwear. "Why?" I asked, as I tried to remember the state of the household laundry pile. It wasn't for any lack. He had just decided to turn in all his superhero underpants. I could not imagine. It was superhero stuff that we had traded in his prop presents for just six months before. "Superheroes are stupid!" he explained. I couldn't believe it. He was moving on, distancing himself from a yearlong obsession. I turned away from my son for a moment of private celebration—Yes!

10

INCH BY INCH

THE MOST RELAXED parent I ever met was a featured speaker at a public health conference, who gave a talk entitled "I Am Too Old for This—Parenting." She was a distinguished academician and researcher in her field of nursing. To establish rapport with her audience, she joked about her life: "I know the reason you all came here today is not to hear about my latest research findings, but to check me out. After all, it is not every day, especially in today's world, that you find a mother of eleven children, all of her own flesh and blood, who is still sane and standing on her own two feet.

"People often ask how we, my husband and I, ever do it, how we have survived. We have been lucky. We both have work that affords us flexibility of hours. We pretty much set our own schedules and can work from home a lot of the time. We take shifts. It took very tight coordination, scheduling, and communication, but we worked it out.

"After the eleventh child, you learn that children pretty much raise themselves. That takes off a lot of the pressure and anxiety that you can put to more productive use . . . You have to have a good sense of humor too and not take yourself too seriously. One day my youngest son, who is six years old, was playing with a friend from school. His older sister was baby-sitting. Then I came home. I overheard my son's friend say, 'I didn't know your grandmother lived with you!' "

The Grandparent Perspective

But often it isn't until we get to grandparenting that we experience the full joy of children. Not being a grandparent myself, I cannot speak from direct experience, but I have heard it so many times that it is worth mentioning.

Gloria, a publisher of children's books and a grandmother, says she wished she could have enjoyed her children more and worried less when they were growing up. "I thought it was my job to control them, which is a big waste because you cannot control them anyway."

After our business meeting, Jackie and I visited about the children in our lives and the joys and struggles of parenting. Suddenly Jackie broke down in tears. "I have gone from therapist to therapist and no one can help me with the guilt I feel . . . I just cannot get rid of it," she said, as if speaking of some adipose tissue on her belly. She reached for a tissue behind her desk. Her daughter had become pregnant at seventeen. "I begged her to abort, I yelled, I screamed . . . but she was adamant about going through with the pregnancy. All my hopes and dreams for my daughter, gone up in smoke." The child in Jackie's life today is a fifteen-month-old grandson. The contortions in her face dissolve as she speaks of him. Clearly, she adores him. "Now I think, 'Oh, my God, what if she had aborted this precious child!'"

Sandy Queen, humorist and parent educator, ended her workshop "The Possible Parent," speaking as a grandparent. Sandy took out from under her blouse a small leather pouch she wears around her neck every day. It contains a small stone and a shell that her two-and-a-half-year-old granddaughter gave her. She held the pouch up for the audience of five hundred people to see. "I have no agenda for my granddaughter," Sandy said, "neither for the time we spend together nor for her life. I am free, and so is she. It took me more than half my life to find it, what is in this pouch . . . unconditional love."[1]

Just as being a parent is an opportunity to revisit our childhood, grandparenting is a chance to revisit our parenting. If there is one phrase that sums up grandparents' words of advice from where they stand on the wheel of life, it is "*relax* and *enjoy!*"

All in Good Time

I have a lot of faith in nature. After all, it put together two human beings inside my womb without any conscious effort on my part. As a pediatric occupational therapist, my eye is finely tuned to the subtleties of child development, the unfolding of nature. When I was a green OT, it wasn't long before I learned to respect my greatest competitor— nature. It beat me in development every time. It was much more powerful and wiser than I could ever hope to be. Therapists and teachers would be bankrupt without it, even though we like to take the credit. I was much more an observer of nature than a manipulator.

As a pediatric occupational therapist, it was always satisfying to teach parents how the different areas of a child's development are often uneven. Some children walk before they talk, and vice versa. It all depends on where the child puts his or her drive, energy, and motivation. It is different for each child. Child development is generic, not specific. Each child's development is like a fingerprint; the basic form is the same, but the detail is like no one else's. Given a healthy body and mind, development will happen all in good time, all in good time.

But even I, the confirmed developmentalist, got caught. My son had shown little interest in paper, pencil, cutting, and drawing skills as a preschooler. When he went to kindergarten, he could write his name—and that was it. His teacher was concerned that he was *just* at age level in fine motor skills. She wanted me to work with him at home on letter formation. I said, "No, when my son is interested he will just run with it; he isn't interested right now. He is focused on other things. I don't want to turn writing into a 'thing.' When he is ready, he will do it." I had a tinge of anxiety, but I knew he was a solid kid. I could wait.

Then in first grade his teacher had a writing center, and the children wrote and illustrated stories. Inventive spelling was encouraged. He proceeded to make a dozen superhero stories that I hard bound into a book.

But when he got to second grade, I panicked. I saw the writing on the wall, the other kids' writing that was displayed in the hallways at school. It was legible, neat, and on the line, and the other kids had many more words at their grasp. I met with his teacher to set up a program or plan. I heard my own words. "He will put it together when he is ready," said his teacher. "Children develop different skills at different rates." I turned red, half from anger and half from embarrassment. At the end of the year, the class wrote business letters to various companies, professional sports teams, and educational and civic organizations for the free promotional stuff they send kids. The letters had to be perfect in format, neatness, spelling, legibility—the works. Well, my son couldn't write enough letters. At last count, he was up to sixty-three. Now he had something he could sink his pencil into.

When children learn things at just the right time, nature's time and their own time, learning is exciting; it is easy; it flows. You can hear the humming as they work. When children are pushed to learn things before they are ready, then they think of learning as hard, frustrating, a struggle. Rote learning looks good and pleases the proud parent, but it does not take the child very far and may dampen his or her love of learning.

One day my son's teacher announced to me that all the students in his class were now readers. Several children had just put the reading process together. What he said next astonished me: "I certainly have no idea how they do it. After twenty years of teaching, it is still a mystery to me. It just seems to happen by combustion. One day they are essentially nonreaders, and the next day they turn a corner, something clicks, and they're off!"

This same phenomenon was reiterated by my daughter's instructor at the pool. "It is amazing. I don't know how kids do it; we try to teach them, but the child has to put it together somehow." At the beginning of the summer, my four-year-old daughter was a nonswimmer; she had to be held, or she would not get in the water. Jumping into the pool was holding onto my arms and reaching for my neck with her legs. At summer's end, she was in the pool for two hours at a time. She neither needed nor wanted me around. She had concocted her own stroke. Butt up, head down, swish, kick, swim.

Inching Out of Competition

So why did I worry? Why did my panic button go off when I saw the displays of students' work hanging in the halls at school? I had not been concerned prior to that; I was comfortable with my son's skills. It was the comparison, the competition. I found that my mind and my body were down on the mat in a wrestling match. Here I was, the disciple of

David Elkind, who espoused that, "Education is not a race; there is no finish line. Healthy education is a life-long process that only comes to an end when we do."[2] I was the one who wanted my son to have the teacher who posted "Education Is Not a Race, It Is a Journey" on his door. My mind, the developmentalist, collided with the distress signals coming from my body.

So relax. You are becoming an overprotective, anxious parent, I told myself. Then it happened again, in soccer. My son was not one of the better players. He was well built and proportioned but small for his age, well coordinated but not a natural athlete, healthy but not aerobically conditioned. He enjoyed playing, but he was not competitive and certainly not aggressive. In fact, he was a bit afraid of getting kicked in the shins.

In his kindergarten year, soccer was just fun for everyone. If the boys remembered which direction to kick the ball, it was a good game. It was in the spring of the second year that the break happened. I could see the more competitive players of the team sailing by my favorite guy. I went into premature labor for his ego. I was puzzled as to why he was not more aggressive. I was off my blanket and shouting to my son to "Get in there," "Get the ball!"—something I had told myself I would never do, after watching the embarrassing behavior of sideline coaching from aggressive parents on other teams. I could see my son smile in amusement on the field. One time when he had a breakaway and was headed down the field, I was jumping, yelling, and raving so wildly that my son broke down laughing, which broke his stride. The ball was intercepted. Thanks, Mom.

I was trying to infuse my son with my competitive spirit. In this situation, it was all wrong. It was causing me to question something about my son. It was clouding my clear picture of him. It was tainting my sacred creed of "no-matter-what-mom." I wanted my husband to practice with him, drill him, get him up to speed. I couldn't care less whether his team won or lost; I just wanted him to get some slaps on the back and high fives too. So much for "All in good time."

Then along came Alfie Kohn, who had the audacity to profess that there is nothing—no, nothing—inherently human or constructive about competition. In fact, Kohn's seven-year research found just the opposite: that competition is inherently destructive, destroys self-esteem, poisons relationships, and causes anxiety. There is no such thing as "healthy competition"; it is an oxymoron. Yikes! This is incredible stuff. But competition is as elemental to American culture as Coke and McDonald's! Kohn said that we have been deluded. The research evidence is all there, in the classroom and the workplace, but it does not get covered in the popular media.[3]

Contrary to common wisdom, Kohn found that competition destroys, rather than builds, self-esteem because it makes a person dependent on the social construct of winning or, as he calls it, *besting* other people. Competition causes anxiety. "When you are trying to beat someone and they're trying to beat you, you are distracted from doing the best job you possibly can," says Kohn. It undermines intrinsic motivation, or the idea of doing something for its own sake.[4]

Child psychologist David Elkind sends out a similar red flag from a different angle. Competition has trickled down to the preschoolers. Today's parents want "superkids." We want them to excel, to achieve. We pass by the earlier stages of development and go straight to competence. Elkind warns parents and educators that pushing academics and competitive sports in the hopes of giving young children an edge and and opportunity to excel can hurt them. He calls it *miseducation*. "Research has shown that children who are not rushed into education are more self-motivated and spontaneous in their learning than the early-learning group. In fact, learning too early dulls a child's interest in learning; it kills their fire." Elkind recommends that we give children the time and space to grow inch by inch, not trying to increase their intelligence through acceleration.[5]

If we want excellence, competition is outmoded. Kohn's research led him to make a startling discovery: "Not only is competition not required for excellence, its absence is required for excellence . . . Researchers have shown repeatedly that cooperation predicts learning more than does competition or individualized attainment . . . the more complicated the task is, the worse competition does, the more cognitive problem-solving and creativity is required, the worse competition stacks up when measured against cooperative approaches."[6]

So what about the soccer game? Kohn advises that we should not get too involved with our children's winning and losing. We should emphasize cooperation, setting up the play, making assists rather than stars.

Competition is a kind of addiction; it gives us that "sweaty sense of accomplishment, that ecstatic feeling of transcendence." We just have not learned another way yet. Kohn believes that "the evidence on competition is so powerful that we should teach kids explicitly about the dangers [of competition] just as we teach about the dangers of alcohol or drugs or driving recklessly."[7]

So where does that leave me? Off the sidelines and back on my blanket. These days when I go to my son's soccer games, I just pretend I'm his grandmother. I sit and watch, bursting with pride, unconditionally. And I elbow my husband to spend some time kicking the soccer ball around with his son.

11

GIFTS

THE DIFFERENCES BETWEEN ourselves and our children are the catalysts for growth spurts of the spirit. They hint at what we will teach each other. Our differences, rather than being a source of tension, are gifts that can lead us into greater wholeness.

A parent for nine years, I have not had my foundation rattled—yet. But I have squared off with difference. I have experienced mini-growth spurts.

In the psychospiritual language of today, we hear about the shadow side, that part of ourselves that is hidden, covered. I like to think of the shadow as the other half of our wholeness. In parenting, it is sometimes our children who cast light on our shadows. Coming out into bright sun from the shade can be uncomfortable at first; it takes a while for our eyes and beings to adjust.

A Son's Gift

My son is a pure-blooded extrovert. By some twist of fate, he was born to a pair of introverted parents. The extroversion/introversion aspect of personality is not a measure of sociability. Introverts can be very outgoing, friendly, and gregarious—like me, for instance. Extroversion/introversion describes the preferred style of refueling one's energy. Extroverts refuel by engaging with others; introverts refuel by being alone or with intimates.[1]

This aspect of personality shows up very early in life. It is tempered by environment, life experience and skills, and stage of life. But the leaning or preference toward extroversion or introversion remains with the person throughout life.

My son, the extrovert, loves to talk. He was an early talker; he wakes up talking, he talks his "think," and he used to follow me into the bathroom to keep on talking. He always bounds through the front door talking. "Hey, Mom!" He was never a child to play by himself; he needs lots of attention. He wants a friend over every day. He loves the group, the team, the club, the class. He loves a crowd and wants to be where the action is: the swimming pool, roller-skating rinks, water parks, ski slopes, parties, airports, the football stadium, and the big city, especially Chicago.

His parents, the introverts, could not be more different. We get our energy or refuel by reading, walking, biking, swimming, running, listening to music, gardening, or writing. To us, a good time is a casual outing with close friends or time with our family. We plan our vacations off-season to avoid the crowds and stay away from big cities. We leave town when there is a big event that floods our city with people and cars. We hate to shop. When we throw a big party, we limit the hours.

The importance of this aspect of personality is paramount in terms of parent-child dynamics. In my parenting classes, it is very illuminating for parents to determine who are the introverts and who are the extroverts in their family. It's an "aha" experience, because there are inherent differences in need and style between the extrovert and the introvert. Just by looking at this one aspect of personality, many family conflicts are uncovered: parent to child, parent to parent, sibling to sibling. The extroverted parent may worry that an introverted child has imaginary friends or does not share what happened at school for a week. An extroverted sister may not respect the privacy needs of an introverted brother. An extroverted wife cannot understand why her introverted husband needs time alone; she takes it as a personal slight.

When we run through all the possible combinations, all participants in my classes agree that the introverted parent with an extroverted child is the most exhausting combo. At times it seems the extroverted child is parasitic, draining the parent of "prana," or life energy.

Before I understood our different styles, I often felt drained by this bursting-wide-open-bundle-of-life son of mine. I was wildly attracted to him; he was so dynamic and magnetic. I loved his exhilarating enthusiasm, his interest in and curiosity about so many things, his nonstop stamina. When I tried to refuel, he was right there, on my lap, in my face, in my space! Bless his heart. Read the newspaper? Forget it. Write in your journal? Ha! Talk on the phone? Not unless he is asleep. Eat a meal uninterrupted? Wait eighteen years.

My extroverted self gets more exercise now. Actually, it has felt good, blood flowing in places that had not been oxygenated. Our son moved me a step, and my husband a whole city block, toward extroversion. We will never be able to do a triathlon in extroversion like running for president of the United States, but we are more balanced introverts and not bad extroverts when we need or want to be.

As Toby's parents, we try to give our extroverted son a healthy diet. He needs both a birthday party and a Halloween party every year; one party is not enough. We all go to the roller rinks, football stadium, water parks, and even Chicago. It's out to dinner every Friday night. He in turn will bike to the football game or student union for a meal; he tells us what to write in the family journal and what's interesting to read in the newspaper. Well, it's a start.

In desperation, my husband, who is a bigger introvert than I, made a brilliant discovery. You can convert the extrovert to introverted activity with a little tenacity. My husband sits in the bathroom and reads the paper while my son talks in the tub; he makes tapes of my son's favorite music that they listen to in the car; they bike when doing errands; they do homework lying on the bed.

Our son, the extrovert, is a gift to our family. Toby is a real get-out-in-the-world kind of guy. He has brought balance to our lives; he has brought the extrovert out in my husband, especially. I never knew my husband could talk so much. Now I know a lot more of what he thinks. My son has drawn out his father's shadow side, his extroverted self, his playfulness, spontaneity, enthusiasm, and humor. What a guy! It was all there, just waiting for his son to pull it out. There are things a parent will do for no other person.

My Daughter's Gift

"Mommy, I want you to be beautiful all the time," said my three-year-old daughter as she supervised my dressing one morning. From the time she was eighteen months old, my daughter surveyed my closet and chose the dress and heels for the day. My usual attire had been jeans, a cotton shirt, and Nikes. She even asked me to put on "lyons," with seamless toes and control top.

From the age of six months, my daughter has loved jewelry. Her interest was inspired by our family helper, Diane, a beautiful woman who wore large, colorful earrings from her impressive collection every day. Diane and Angela had a ritual every morning. Immediately after Diane hung up her coat, she would sweep Angela into her arms. Angela got a close look at Diane's earrings and touched them, ever so delicately. When Angela was a year old, Diane took off her earrings and clipped them on Angela's ears. Together they would go to the bathroom for a good look in the mirror. By age two, Angela had her own jewelry.

Never would I have anticipated such sheer feminine tastes from a child at such a young age. I believed femininity was a learned behavior. But it was absolutely clear from a very young age that my daughter was into beauty. She just came that way. It didn't stop at jewelry. Then came the dresses and party shoes and hair bows. My daughter would always choose clothing and jewelry over toys, but shoes were her absolute passion. Whenever we went into a department store, we somehow always gravitated to the shoe department. Once we found her size in the shoe rack, she was down on the floor trading in her own for the pairs with bows, sparkles, fancy laces, Disney characters, slip-ons . . . If we had the time, she could be occupied for an hour. One morning, when my husband needed to borrow my daughter's whistle for a presentation he was giving that day, she would not give it up. In desperation, he bribed her: "Angela, I'll get you a new pair of shoes." Without hesitation, she handed over the whistle.

Angela did not get this from me, at least not on the surface. I too am into beauty, but not the kind that comes from makeup. I am a minimalist in that department. Fashion was not my forte, and my accessories were, shall I say, ancillary. I just didn't have the time. I keep my hairstyle easy and breezy. I was into low-maintenance living, both for myself and for my home. If I had time for myself, it went to reading, walking, writing, teaching, and time with friends. My motto was "What you see is what you get." I had grown up during the feminist era and under the banner: Serious women do not focus on beauty. Real women develop their minds.

So I have a daughter who is into beauty. It was not learned. She just came that way. She showed me my shadow side. I've had my moments of high beauty and generally thought of myself as attractive when I put some effort into it. Fact is, I would just like to rise in the morning, shower, brush my teeth and hair, put on my clothes, and look as good as those evenly tanned, flat-bellied, smooth-skinned, shapely lifeguards at the pool. I'm sure that is all they do. They are no Barbie® dolls; they are real people. They teach my kids how to swim.

My daughter's wish, "Mommy, I want you to be beautiful all the time," stirred something in me. I chose not to view my daughter's request as just another cute comment that kids make, but as a wake-up call. I knew the only way she would retain her value of beauty was if I honored mine. I was enough of a parent to know that you don't get very far with just talk. Modeling has power in parenting.

I remember my amazement at the confession of one of my professors in graduate school. Dr. Carpenter was a strong and outspoken feminist. But there was one thing that did not fit. She was a self-made beauty and obviously self-conscious about the way she looked. She kept her beautiful auburn hair long and wore it in a variety of styles that were not low maintenance. Once she joined me in the ladies' room before class to freshen up her makeup and hair. Dr. Carpenter once told the class that she always has to watch her weight and was within five pounds of her goal. Someone in the class blurted out, "You! Gee, you always look great!" Laughing, Dr. Carpenter leaned against her desk. "It hasn't always been that way," she said. She went on to explain: "As a professor and lecturer, I ask people to look at me. I ask for their attention. I believe it is my responsibility to give them something good to look at." So that's how she gets around it, I thought. It's part of her job. And now here I was telling myself that it was my job, as my daughter's mother, to be beautiful, at least more of the time.

There were other memories. A bunch of us were shooting the breeze in the dorm dining room after dinner. We, college men and women, were discussing the then-prominent women's movement and the ascent of women. Our supportive male friends were giving us feedback, their views. I do not remember the details of the conversation except for one statement that percolated to the top of all the chatter from both sides. "Smart women take care of their beauty; they attend to it. It is part of their power." At the time, I did not react to this defensively, as a sexist, anti-feminist statement. I just listened and felt strangely grateful. This statement cut through all the ideology that we were all trying on for size and digesting to varying degrees. This one statement rose out of the fray. I recognized it as truth. I never forgot it. This young man knew that women were meant to be the keepers of beauty. It was no insignificant matter. It was universal and timeless.

Years later I found, somewhat to my surprise, that my husband was of like mind. He had always been very supportive of women professionally and had opened doors for many. One year we lived in Chapel Hill, North Carolina, a beautiful college town that was both southern in charm and modern in pace. During that year, my husband commented now and again how refreshing he found the southern women. "What do you mean?" I asked. "Well, they seem to really enjoy being women; they know how to take care of themselves. They really care how they look." At my coaxing, he elaborated. "Northern women seem to hide or disguise themselves as men; southern women seem to like being women." I think it was a kind of awakening for him. He, too, had come of age during the feminist era. He had circulated with serious women.

Back to my daughter. Angela liked to go to preschool all

dressed up in her fancy dresses and party shoes and the five-dollar-and-up hair bows. I found myself half apologizing to the other preschool mothers, whose daughters wore play clothes and pigtails: "No, she did not just come from a birthday party; this is all she will wear." I was the helpless accomplice. Actually, I was just letting her be herself.

On her fourth birthday party in the first week in January, when it was fifteen degrees below zero, out from under the heavy snowsuits came seven little girls all dressed in frilly party dresses, patent-leather shiny shoes and five-dollars-and-up bows in their hair. I literally did not recognize one of my daughter's friends.

When I called my mother that afternoon to share the party news and all the fancy dress-up at fifteen degrees below zero, she laughed and said, "Angela had a coup. She set a standard, and they all aspired to it. I can think of no better way for Angela's friends to honor her on her birthday! You know, Linda," my mother paused, "you were just the same way as a child, extremely feminine, very fancy. You had to be just so."

So on my fortieth birthday, I decided to pull a coup of my own. I went shopping and came home with an elegant, full-length, sleek, bare-backed, black evening gown, long gloves, rhinestone dangling earrings, and top-of-the-line patent-leather heels. I had my hair done in a soft French twist. It was high beauty time. My husband and I dined at the most elegant restaurant in town. Afterwards, we went dancing. As I was getting dressed for the evening, my daughter was beside herself, jumping all around the room like my private cheerleader.

It was my daughter's beauty that prompted me to take another look in the mirror. After all, she did come from me. It was my daughter who pulled my beauty, which had been hidden under the shade, out into the light. The shade had been created by my particular time of coming of age.

We can take these wake-up calls from our children because they have no motivation. By just being themselves, they cast light on our shadow side, the other side of our wholeness. Our children want us to stop hiding from our own magnificence, to stop pruning ourselves with such things as temperament types or the dogma of social movements that we have either already outgrown or need to outgrow.

12

ONE ON ONE

A FAMILY IS more than the sum of its parts. It is the sum of its relationships. A family of a mother, father, son, and daughter is not a family of four; it is a family of six. A family with a mother, father, two daughters, and one son is a family of ten. And a family with a mother, father, and five children is a family of twenty-one.

New math? No. Just new thinking. A family is made up of the number of relationships rather than the number of members.

Here is how you add it up. A family of a mother (M), father (F), son (S), and daughter (D) includes the following distinct relationships: M-F, M-S, M-D, F-S, F-D, and S-D. Add one more member, and the number of relationships goes up by four, so that a family of five members has ten different relationships.

Last year we had a family reunion on my husband's side. There were fourteen members of the extended family, which involved over ninety different relationships.

Keeping Intimacy Alive with Our Children

As parents, we think we are in the business of raising children. I think parents are in the business of raising relationships. Parents are setting a standard for all future relationships in their child's life. According to psychologist Harville Hendrix, author of *Getting the Love You Want,* we were unconsciously attracted to our mates because they reminded us of our parents.[1]

Deep, intimate relationships take one-on-one. Usually we tend to reserve this level of intimacy for our mate or lover, but it applies to the parent-child and all other relationships as well.

We only have enough time and energy to be in intimate relationships with just so many people. The life cycle and life circumstance put us into deep relationships with people on a temporary basis. Some circle back, and some never do. For example, siblings live, play, squabble, and grow up together. They may or may not grow apart by distance or lifestyle. It also happens that siblings consider each other best friends, or they become the most trusted business partners.

The parent-and-child relationship needs to bond not just once at birth but over and over. The parent-child relationship stays close through one-on-one rebonding. This is especially true between mother-son and father-daughter. You cannot count on living under the same roof to suffice for keeping you together in close relationship. There are the inevitable differences in interests and choice of activities. But it doesn't have to be that way. I can remember my mother telling me that my Grandma Nellie always stayed up on the ratings of professional baseball and football teams so she would always have something to talk to her grown son about. Now, thirty-five years later, I find myself in the same spot, not with my adult son but with a mere eight-year-old. He loves to talk sports; he keeps track of them all. To say I am marginally interested is an exaggeration. I really am only interested when he is on the field.

So I have a choice. I can pretend to be interested in sports, or I can try to find something of mutual interest. Here's my solution: I will throw and catch in a beautiful park, go skating on outdoor rinks, and ski on picturesque slopes. I will bike on the lake shore bike path and swim in the tree-enclosed outdoor pool. The perfect match: my passion for the outdoors and his for sport. As a return on my agreement to spend a day driving to see the Green Bay Packers Hall of Fame, he goes on a scenic boat ride with stops to walk through the caverns of the beautiful Wisconsin Dells. We can each give a day to share each other's passion. It provides balance in a relationship. That is why the buggy for biking and the baby joggers are so popular; they provide balance and build intimacy between parent and child.

As for my daughter, she is a breeze. She is still young and very much into the explorative stage, so open; everything is worth at least one look. Remember that magical time? So far, I think she will share my love of flowers, animals, and water and I will relish in sharing her love of beauty and creative arts.

Out of Role

It is so easy to fall into the father-takes-the-son and the mother-takes-the-daughter routine. There is less tension, less work. There is also great loss for all involved.

The son misses intimacy with his mother and the opportunity to communicate with a woman. It is important that a son know his mom beyond the minister of laundry and lunches, chauffeur and chef. His mother is an interesting person in her own right. She has a sharp wit, she is a mean roller blader, and she knows how to pronounce all those French words in the restaurant. There will never be a woman more proud to be on his arm or who is more intensely interested in anything he wants to tell her. She is the only person who knows his history better than he does.

Now as for father and daughter, she will know what it feels like to be absolutely adored by a man. He will take great pleasure in pleasing her in tangible ways like wearing the gaudy tie she sewed for him in Brownies, sending flowers addressed to her, or buying tickets to the ballet. He will coach her soccer team and go to her swim meets, as well as compliment her pretty hair and stunning outfit. He will put down his newspaper and listen to a essay or book report and make some constructive comments that get her an A. He will purposely act a little dumb about things that she knows about as a ploy to let her show off a bit.

There is usually one parent the children spend more time with—Mom. Even so, if there is more than one child in the family, time alone with Mom is at a premium. Time spent with Dad is more often spent with Mom and Dad together. So one-on-one time with Dad is still rarer. Dad becomes the missed parent, even if the family is intact and all living under one roof.

My friend Susan has three sons between the ages of five and twelve. She takes time to be alone with each son every week for at least an hour or so, even if it is just going for a bike ride or a walk in the neighborhood, to the library, or meeting for lunch at home. Once a month Susan and son try to do something special, like going out for a movie and pizza or taking a trip to visit relatives, just the two of them. "This is the only way I have come up with to really keep in touch with each one of my sons," said Susan. "Otherwise, they just all sort of blur together."

Taking time to be one-on-one with each child removes the roles that both child and parent tend to fall into when in the whole family system. The child can step out of sex and birth-order roles: brother, sister, boy, girl, oldest, middle, or youngest child. The same is true for Mom and Dad; we play our respective roles. Every family is different. The healthiest families exchange roles from time to time and can assume each other's roles if necessary. But we have all grown comfortable in our special areas of expertise. We defer to our parent-partner in certain areas or when we are tired of making decisions. "Ask your Mom, that is her department." "Go ask Dad, I'm busy right now." Our roles can limit our connection or relatedness to each individual family member unless we take a break from them for a while.

An Investment with Dividends

This summer, my son and I spent a weekend together at water park heaven. On the first day we just played. The second day we dug each other. Without the family dynamics that two other members inevitably add, we spent much less time discussing what, when, and how. There was more time and energy to just enjoy each other. Flexibility flourished; there was less territory to protect. Two can bend much better than four. I felt much freer, free of my role as mediator of all the family negotiations. I felt free from having to divide my attention between two children. I relished the luxury of that one-on-one focus without multiple distractions. I could witness firsthand my son's maturity as he worked the locker that I couldn't open, read the map to navigate through the six-acre park, and handled his own money at mealtime. He in turn was the beneficiary of his mother's altruistic grit or foolishness in waiting in the full sun at high noon for one hour to take the new and infamous Kowabunga speed water slide ride. At the top of our ascent was a sign that read "This is an aggressive ride; if you are pregnant or have back problems or heart disease, do not proceed." "Does sunstroke count?" I wondered. The ride was over in fifteen seconds.

When we returned home, father and daughter had had their own fling. My daughter proudly showed me her sparkling new nails that she had professionally painted with a tiny rhinestone painted on each pinky finger. That was just the beginning.

These one-on-one times have their lasting effects. You get multiple returns on your investment. My relationship with my son held less tension and conflict once we had spent some time together. We were back in sync. The tension between us was his frustration in not getting enough of my attention and my sense that I was shortchanging him somehow. He needed time with me, just me. He was tired of having to fight for it. Fight his sister, fight my work, fight the phone, fight the errands . . .

Father and daughter are more hooked in and seem to have more to share. I hear more "Dad" calling and more dialogue between them. I see more father-daughter flirting and playfulness. When Dad comes home, Angela vanishes. She is swarming her father. Not long after their weekend together, I heard Angela ask her father, "Are you happy I came back to you?"

It is important for mother-daughter and father-son to have their times together too. Father and son can take that canoe trip and camp in the wilderness; they can hike the mountain ranges and rock climb. They can go to the big stadium and watch the pros play ball. Male bonding. Just the guys.

Mothers and daughters need that time too. They can shop in the city, lunch at a favorite café, or take a walk in a wildlife sanctuary. They can do whatever nurtures their souls and relationship without the intrusion from their male counterparts. Mother-daughter bonding. Just the girls.

It is during the one-on-one times that a child will share some of the deeper layers of his or her being with the trusted parent. Riding alone in the car is one of those times. There are no distractions, and the motion seems to relax the body and mind enough to unleash the brewing questions that a child's supple mind is pondering. When my daughter was four and a half, she asked, "Do four-year-olds ever die before they reach five?" She had been asking a lot about death. "What do dead people look like? What happens to you when you die? Who has died in our family? When will I die?" Talking about other people's deaths or old people's deaths was within my comfort zone, but when she asked about her own, I was startled. I checked in with my favorite pediatrician, her father, and found out she was developmentally on target.

Almost every night, my husband and I have one-on-one time with our children. We unplug the phone and put down the day. Since we have never had a problem getting our children to bed, the only down side is that they are addicted to this special time, even when Mom and Dad are bushed and want to take a raincheck or when the baby-sitter comes. Our usual one-on-one time is spent in very ordinary ways: reading aloud, a game, a bath, or a special TV program. I like to think of it as smoothing out the ruffles to the day. If the day ends well, you sleep well and get up well.

One-on-One with Adult Children

These times together will be the points of connection later in life when parent and child no longer live under one roof or in the same city. The fishing trip or golf game with Dad may be critical for a struggling adult son who needs some perspective and counsel from his experienced father. It is much more likely that the son will share while pitching the tent or putting on the green than over the phone or in the living room at holiday family gatherings. The same is true for mother and daughter: "Mom, tell me about . . . " over coffee at the bookstore café, or during a walk by the lake.

Adult children want to hear their parents' stories. It is in the telling that the adult child finds what he or she is looking for: the guiding values, the struggle, the decision-making process, the choices, the missing pieces, and the perspective. The adult children have stories to tell too. By hearing themselves talk, by having a wholehearted listener, one who has their best interest in mind, adult children will know what to do, not because their parents told them, but because the children have heard their own words, their own counsel.

I learned this from a woman in her early sixties, an attractive woman with soft blond hair done in a stylish bun, soft wrinkles, and gentle eyes. She and I had both accompanied our husbands to a conference. She was waiting on a bench outside a large lecture hall. As I approached, she invited me to sit down. We introduced ourselves. Not knowing how much time we had before our husbands would appear, I asked about her children. (I am always looking for parenting stories from the other end of the spectrum.) She had five grown children. They were all doing well and were reasonably happy. "How did you do it?" I asked. (I like to do my research on success cases.) "Oh," she chuckled, "I don't know, you just do what you have to do." "No, I mean, how did you *raise* them?" I asked. She hesitated for a minute. "I guess I did a lot of listening. I still do, for that matter." She looked at me. Her eyes were clear. "How so?" I asked. "Well, they will call home and want to talk, so I listen and just ask some questions. They don't need me to give them advice; they need me to listen so they can hear themselves talk. I always know when they know what to do. They'll say, "Well, I've got to go; thanks, Mom." She must have known the secret of one-on-one.

13

THINK AND BECOME

"YOU MUST THINK of her as a normal child and treat her accordingly. She has a mechanical defect that can be corrected, that's all."

The parents were drilled with clear instructions for how they were to treat their daughter, born with congenital heart disease. Treat her as a normal, healthy child. If they could do that, leave their fears and anxiety off of her, then they had met their responsibilities.

At first glance, this may sound patronizing to concerned parents. But looking more deeply, the message is, "We, the doctors, have the easy part: correcting the heart organ. It is your job as her parents to protect her psyche. Do not give her any messages that she is weak or needs special protection beyond what you would give a normal child. We can repair the heart, but a weakened psyche may have a lifelong effect."

The parents did a very good job. Just one month before the girl had surgery at the age of ten, she won the fifty-yard dash in field day at her school. She was never restrained from any physical activity. In fact, she was encouraged to do as much as she wanted: running, biking, swimming, skating, skiing, sledding. The school was alerted that she was not to be restricted on the playground or in gym. The only restrictions would be self-imposed.

This is a thirty-five-year-old story. Despite my parents' great work, I did not pass through without a scar. It was the daylong cardiology checkups every six months, as far back as my memory went, in a big, dark, old hospital that smelled like antiseptic alcohol. Then came the surgery itself. The intensive care with all its beepers and horrible sucking sounds, the drainage tubes coming out of my body, the oxygen tent that they wanted to put me in, the frozen shoulder from holding my arm against my incision, and the scar that runs all around my shoulder blade. Not the stuff of normal childhood.

My heart became my weak spot. It was where I displaced my pain. Whenever I did not want to look at my pain or had no one at hand whom I trusted enough with it, I buried it in my chest.

During a time of real heartache in my life, I went to a cardiologist because of chest pain. The doctor was baffled. "I do not know what is causing your chest pain. I do know that it is not from heart disease like angina or a heart attack, 99 percent sure." This doctor did not send me away. He read my lack of reassurance. "What can I do to prove to you that your chest pain is not from your heart?" he asked. I rattled off the tests I wanted done. He agreed. When I returned for the tests, he attended them all instead of just getting a printout of the results on his desk to review. He "oohed" and "aahed" when reading the little jagged lines on the monitors. "You have a very functional heart. I'm not going to tell you it is perfect, but it works well. I know many people who would die, I mean, would be thrilled, to have your heart." He echoed the words of my pediatric cardiologist decades before: "It is important that you do not think of yourself as having heart disease. It is important to think of your heart as healed."

I left the appointment with a load off my chest. I no longer had to carry the fear of something being wrong in my vulnerable spot. This cardiologist was also a healer, whether he knew it or not. He used the tools available to him to excise my fear and anxiety. That was the end of my chest pain.

Not only does the field of medicine know about thinking and being (even though doctors come at it sideways), but the field of education does as well. One of the landmark discoveries in the field of education, the "self-fulfilling prophecy," found that students perform according to their teachers' expectations. When a teacher previews an incoming student's true or counterfeit academic record, the student will perform accordingly. Unintentional bias can also come from other teachers, prior reputation, or siblings.

Several years ago I was looking for the creative writing papers I did in high school. I came across a manila folder labeled "Linda" in the file cabinet in my parents' home. No papers. What I did find was a complete record of my public school education. What a chance, K-12 at a glance. I felt a little guilty snooping into the "private" documents (report cards) of my child self. What I found was so obvious and so consistent throughout my school years that it was irrefutable: excellence begets excellence; mediocrity begets mediocrity. In classes where I liked and respected the teachers (which, translated, means that they respected and liked children and their profession), I received high marks and glowing comments. In classes where I did not particularly like the teachers and did not like their teaching (they usually went hand in hand), my marks fell to the grade I would probably have given the teacher myself if I felt generous on grading day.

Last summer, my family rented a cottage from a retired

couple who had both been teachers, she in public education and he in higher education. We had never met. Our business was all carried out long distance. In the closet-sized upstairs bath, over the sink, was a small primitive art sign. The painted lettering had faded, but I could make it out by leaning in close: "A teacher touches the life of a child forever." I knew what kind of teacher she was.

Parenting Field

I believe children take in much more of what we think and feel and much less of what we say. They are adept mind and emotion readers. Children let us know what they pick up from us by their behavior. If we are suppressing anger, they will act it out for us. If we feel great, they will give us a I-love-you hug. If we are anxious, they will whine. If we are worried, they will withdraw.

I also believe that children become to some degree what their parents or any adult they are bonded to thinks of them. Placement in the family is a good example. It is common for the firstborn to be the high achiever because of the parents' expectation and projection of their own agendas onto the child. We had a baby-sitter for two years who was a classic firstborn. Megan was attending graduate school in statistics at the university. She still had time for singing in a soft-rock quartet and two part-time jobs. In just two years, Megan found her mate, graduated, married, bought and renovated a house, and found a great job in her field. I told her she was a classic first child, a perfect example of the fast-forward syndrome. She agreed. At her wedding, Megan's mother confirmed the diagnosis.

Children are thin-minded; their membranes are easily penetrable. By this I mean they pick up, as if by osmosis, what we are thinking and feeling, most specifically about them. Our children do not just take in our words. I've learned that a parent cannot camouflage their speech. Our children get the message anyway.

Just a minute before, I had told my son, "Don't read the paper at the table. You'll spill your milk." And he did. He was looking at the paper and not watching where he was reaching. I felt like saying, "Oh, come on!" or "I told you so." By some miracle, the mantra "natural consequences, natural consequences, natural consequences" stopped me. "Get a paper towel and clean it up," I said. I took a deep sigh and whisked the soaked place mat off the table. My irritation was leaking out all over. All of a sudden, my son started wailing, "I'm dumb, I'm just soooo dumb." I was horrified. "No, you aren't!" I retorted. My tone had radically changed. My son continued his recitation. He was on a roll. I noticed a little suppressed smile as he swiped at the spill with the paper towel. He beat me, and we both knew it. I mimicked his chant. He fell to the floor holding his stomach and kicking in laughter. I rest my case.

On his first day of golf lessons, my son was getting some pointers from another mom, who was a seasoned golfer. The kids had finished the formal part of the lesson, hitting the ball on the driving range with the pros. Now it was time for the parents to take them around a couple of holes. I couldn't help him much, since I have played only nine holes of golf in my life. When we started out, I pointed to the tee and called out to my son, "You tee off on the green." The woman looked at me sideways and said as we were passing by the flag, "This is the green. That," she pointed up the hill, "is the tee off." At that point I guess she figured she had better help this poor lad or his well-meaning but misled mother would get him totally confused.

Down the fairway from hole number two was a pond. At the tee off, my son dug his toe into the turf and said, "I will probably hit into the water." "Don't think that or you will," said the golf-pro-mom. "It always happens to me, at least." I thought to myself, "Now I could have told him that, and I don't even golf."

Think and They Become. It can be a harrowing idea. "Awesome," as our kids say. I know, I know. We parents are just getting our act together in terms of behavioral techniques and language. Now we have to get our thoughts in line too? Certainly one's mind is the private realm of self, where one can satisfy one's urges in fantasy without having to act them out in reality—like running away from home, or throwing the kids into next week, or changing them into gerbils.

But thoughts do carry an energy that can be positive or negative. That energy is what you feel when you walk into someone's home or office. It is inviting; it feels good. It has good vibes, or it doesn't.

Certainly our thoughts cannot change our children into gerbils or gorgeous geniuses. Children are not moldable in our minds. It's not that easy. But our thinking carries a backdrop that becomes part of our child's environment. Our thoughts are part of the many influences that come into play that either serve and support our children or subvert them.

To the Rescue

This idea of Think and Become as related to parenting came to me loud and clear two years ago when we were vacationing on Lake Superior with some friends. My family had taken the ferry out to one of the Apostle Islands that was noted for its beautiful hiking trails and looming stretches of white, sandy beaches that are shallow over one hundred feet out, perfect for young children.

Our friends were going to meet up with us on Stockton Island. They had rented a small motorboat; we took the ferry. After an unbearable time on the beach (the black flies were biting bad), we headed back to the docks on the other end of the island to catch the last ferry run of the day. Halfway back, my friend Beth asked Toby if he would like to ride back with them in their motorboat. I was not prepared for this and hesitated. "Ah, well . . . you have an extra small life jacket?" They did. Ignoring me, Beth repeated her question, "Toby, would you like to come with us?" At first he was wild about the idea. Then he probably picked up on my rummaging mind and emotions. I was trying very hard to let him be free to go if he wanted. "Should I go, Mom? What do you think, Mom?" His dependence on me crawled all over me like the black flies back at the beach. What is the bottom line here? I asked myself. The winds were high, the water very choppy, but the sun was shining, and there was no threatening weather on the horizon. But Lake Superior is notorious for its sudden and volatile weather changes and patterns. We had just the day before seen all the pictures of the shipwrecks at the National Forest Headquarters in Bayfield. My mind switched. What is the bottom line here? Do I trust my friends and their judgment? I asked myself. Yes. I turned to my son and said, "I think it would be great fun. You will be safe with Beth and Mike." "Okay, I'll go," he said, as he kicked the rocks on the trail in front of him as if to finalize the decision.

When we got to the dock, the boat was smaller than I had thought. I looked for a radio but did not see one. It must be in the compartment, I told myself. Beth and Mike got under way before the ferry, and I waved to Toby from the dock. My heart was in my throat as they headed out into the open lake, the second largest in the world. I watched the boat splash as it hit the crests of the waves and thought, That is going to be a rough ride back. After the ferry got under way, I fixed my sight on my friends' small craft that we were catching rapidly. I changed seating three times so that I could keep my eyes on the boat that all too soon became a speck. "My son is out there," I thought, "open to this ocean-lake." I was drowning in my own anxiety.

I finally sat down and resigned myself to the rest of the trip, just hoping it would get over with fast. The scenery did nothing for me. I noticed there were no other craft out on the lake. My husband was standing up in the lower deck, leaning against the side of the boat, silent as if seasick. Just as we were making our approach into the mainland, a Coast Guard boat shot away from the pier and headed toward us at full speed ahead. All the passengers on the crowded ferry took notice. The voice of our captain came over the loudspeaker. "There must be a boat in distress; the Coast Guard never speeds away like that when it's just making its rounds." I swiveled around to see if any craft were in sight. The Coast Guard boat was heading in the direction from where we had just come. Oh, my God!

The captain of the ferry volunteered that he could not pick up any radio distress calls. As soon as we were docked, my husband and I ran to the Coast Guard headquarters, located on a pier just behind our hotel. My daughter started to cry because of the rough ride in our arms.

I went to the window and asked the guard on duty about the call. She said a small craft had capsized. I somehow got the next question out: "Can you give us more information?" "Why do you need to know?" the young woman asked, with irritation in her voice. I explained that our six-year-old son was on a small boat on his way back from the islands. I hated to explain, as if this somehow made it a reality. Her face changed; she radioed to someone and nodded as she received communication back. "Thank you, over and out." She looked up at me and said, "It was a sailboat, Ma'am." I suddenly felt very tired, absolutely wrung out.

Close call. Let this be a warning. Be careful what you think.

Unsticking Stuck Stuff

In *Liberated Parent, Liberated Child*, Adele Faber and Elaine Mazlish review some of the roles we cast our children in: Mr. Sad Sack, The Princess, The Whiner. The authors make the point that it is our own labeling, our own typecasting, and our own attitudes (our "think") that create (become) these roles. We get ourselves and our children unstuck by changing our "think," our language, and our attitudes.[1]

Charlotte, a friend who had taken a Faber/Mazlish parent training course, told me that her own parents had typecast her as the "creative one" and her sister as the "brainy one." "This limited both of us," Charlotte said.

Beyond getting the limiting and labeling stuff out of our children's way, we can use Think and Become to bolster our children's lives. We can strengthen, rather than stifle, their magnificence.

A Little Story

My son was frustrated. He hadn't had a chance to score all season. His morale was down, and there were only a couple of games left. I was worried he would give up on himself and maybe "turn off" on soccer. Before he left for a game with his dad one afternoon, I said, "Toby, today I think you'll take a shot at the goal." "You really think so?" he asked. There was hope in his voice. "Yes," is all I said.

After the game, Toby yelled out to me as he crashed open the front door. "Hey, Mom, guess what happened? I made an assist!"

In the world that his generation must learn to create for their own survival, the world of cooperation, an assist is as good as a goal.

Our thoughts can be either a boost or a bother to our children and ourselves. Think and Become is like a Hippocratic Oath for parents: Above all, do no harm. What we think about our children is part of the parenting package. To know that our thoughts have energy, that they have power and influence, is to also know more about ourselves. It is to know another way to safeguard our children's wholeness and recapture our own.

14

PASSING ON PASSION

CHILDREN KNOW US best by our passions. Passion is spirit singing through. If parents have a passion, our children will want one too. Parent and child can get hooked on each other's passions. They can share and trade.

At age two, my son got his family totally wrapped up in trucks. Truck hunts to construction sites became a favorite family outing. Jumping ahead five years and over many other passions, my son accomplished the ultimate. He got Mom into football. This was a miracle. When my mother came to visit she even took pictures of me watching a football game on television as evidence to show to my two older brothers. "They will never believe me," she explained. As a child, I used to fold my arms and pout during Sunday afternoon football. You know, it was boring and stupid. Now, as a parent, I took another look and tried to find an angle. I am into biography, so okay, I got interested in some players. It wasn't long before my son caught on. "Hey, Mom, Dan Marino is on!" he called from the basement.

Passion is contagious, infectious, and wholehearted. At the very least, it gets our attention. It wasn't long before I realized that this is how a child learns best. A child with a passion doesn't just *like* trucks, Peter Pan, or football; he takes on the role, gets in the driver's seat, puts on the costume or uniform, and soaks everything out of it. Each passion organically leads to another. A passion for pirates led us to Peter Pan, which led to flying, which led to space. Every night Toby and his dad "went into space" as they pored over space books, the solar system, the Milky Way, Universe Number One.

We learn most from doing, becoming. Adults call it pretending. It seems like nothing more than play. Years ago I saw a movie about the scientists F. H. C. Crick and James D. Watson, who discovered the configuration of DNA as the double helix. With the knowledge of top scientists, they searched together in their minds at every chance, combing the beautiful campus of Cambridge like two boys on a scavenger hunt. They spoke of the DNA molecule as a playmate that was hiding, and they were "it." The breakthrough came when they asked each other, "If we were a DNA molecule, what would we look like?"

Back to football. I have a bias against spectator sports and spectator living. One of the risks in growing up is that we become more spectator and less doer. That was my beef with football. To my surprise, football has not been all brawn and no brain. It was football that taught my son the rudiments of arithmetic with adding and subtracting yardage and scores. It got him acquainted with the daily newspapers and created at least the once-a-day-reading-ritual of the sports section. It taught him United States geography, in locating the home states and towns of teams, and it even taught him to write neat and legible business letters to players and teams for autographs and team paraphernalia. Not bad.

Passion as Teacher

When you are hooked on a passion, learning is spontaneous, natural, effortless. It just happens; you cannot hold it back even if you want to. Passion is not for the spectator; passion is totally active. It engages the whole person. In my family, I try to keep spectators off the bench. My son needs to know that touchdowns and field goals do not just happen like instant replays. So we toss the football around. It is his constant companion; just don't break the lamps, please. We try to kick, pass, throw, spiral, run with agility, and break away. We test the body and try it out in new ways. What else can I do with this fantastic machine of mine?

Beyond the physical play, sports makes for male-to-male bonding. Guys have a language all their own—sports talk. It seems to be universal. Sports can be an instant icebreaker and warm-up for both boys and men. I repent. I can see as a mother what I did not see as a daughter and sister.

In ideal circumstances, teachers do not "teach"; they are creators of learning. They create the circumstances that allow learning to happen. In an environment rich in medium and diverse in approach, the student learns by osmosis. (I call it "osmotic learning.") The student naturally gravitates to the learning activities that are the best fit for his learning style, strengths, and stage of development.

Only Mr. Struglia could get you interested in an amoeba. In his booming baritone voice, he serenaded down the halls every morning singing his Biology 101 greatest hits, as we fumbled with the debris falling out of our lockers and onto our heads. If your learning style was not in the auditory range, he covered the visual as well. He paid junior high students to walk up and down the high school wing with colorful poster board, with diagrams on the front, lyrics on the back. I think he thought that if it rhymed, we could remember it better. If you were a kinesthetic learner, dissection was on Tuesdays. Mr. Struglia was ahead of his time.

My son's first-grade teacher was not just hands on; she was turned on! The energy and enthusiasm she brought to her classroom were exceptional. Creating rich and diverse learning activities for children was her passion. The children did not learn to read in reading groups; they learned to read by acting out stories and writing their own. Instead of measuring lines on an arithmetic paper, they measured out dinosaurs in the hallway with a surveyor's wheel. Once I asked her how she did it. "I am as excited about learning as the kids are. I love to learn new things, and that is what I bring to the classroom . . . People ask me how I maintain such an enthusiastic, open, young attitude toward life. It is from being around kids all day; I catch it from them," she said.

A parent's passion seems to get passed through the genes. My friend Kathy loves physical activity. It is her passion. Every weekend is devoted to bike trips, tennis matches, or skiing, depending on the season. Kathy runs every day, year round. I chuckle when Kathy complains that her daughter, Madeleine, wears her out. From day one, Madeleine has wanted to *be* motion. Kathy complains that when she would expect her daughter to be tired, worn out from physical exertion, "She just gets more fit." Despite her eight short years, Madeleine is a competitive swimmer, can keep up with her parents in cross-country skiing and twenty-mile bike trips, does elementary jumps in figure skating, and is a skillful gymnast for her age.

Peak Experience

Passion is a great teacher. It teaches us how to live within the fullness and wholeness of life. Passion engages all of us, our whole mind, body, and spirit. When we are doing our passion, we feel right with ourselves and right with the world. We feel that oneness that we have come to call *peak experience*. I believe childhood is full of peak experiences. That is why we look back at that time in our lives (if we had the luxury of having a true childhood) with such fondness and longing. Just watch any child play—the total absorption, the sparkle in her eyes, the joy in his voice, the freedom of her movements.

John Parera-Villalva knows about passion. In the first half of his life, he was a jet-setting businessman, selling plastics around the world. He was successful. He retired early and returned to the art of his Portuguese father, sculpting. He had the background and talent. He updated himself with some courses and is on his second successful career. His daughter, Diane Nuttycombe, shared with me his promotional postcard. On the back were these words: "My work takes me away from worldly turmoil and into a state of quiet creativity that enriches and frees me from institution and format. It integrates perfectly with my faith, my God and creation. It is the essence of life."

Do passion and peak experiences have to be sacrificed to growing up? I think that is what worried Peter Pan. This eternal youth had to create his own world of Never-Never Land. For what? To be away from adults? To be free to do whatever he wanted? To hold onto his passion for play? Maybe. But I believe that he was running away to be free of self-consciousness. When children become self-conscious, we see less abandoned play. They want to be private in their play, and when an adult enters the room the bubble is broken. Or when they enter school and performance becomes primary, osmotic learning, abandoned learning is lost. We separate from oneness and into self-consciousness. We are out of ourselves, always checking on ourselves.

Oneness, the loss of self-consciousness, is possible through passion. For me that means being with my family, making love, communing with nature, and sometimes writing and teaching. There is never any guarantee. It just seems to happen by chance, spontaneously. It was a great class. I was on, and the class clicked. There was chemistry; sometimes you get it, and sometimes you don't. On good writing days, I feel inspired or am inspired by what I wrote. It was a great date, crowned with transcendent lovemaking. The kids and Mom are in a good mood, we frolic, laugh, play.

It took me years, really half a lifetime, to realize that what I thought could only happen by chance, could be created by my own intention, at least more of the time. Now before I "teach," I do my usual preparation, review, updating, and revision. When in class, I try to focus off myself and onto my students. I get them to talk. I hear their issues, and I try to rewrap the class package to be in the best service of the class needs. That is when the magic happens. I say things I never knew that I knew, and class participants say things that inspire everyone. The class is in flow. The feeling comes and goes. It takes tremendous focus, trust, and willingness to let go of control. It takes courage to lose self-consciousness, to give your whole self over and surrender. That is when we feel the passion, the rush, the high, the bliss.

Going Places with Passion

Passion can take you places too. When I was a child, my mother's passion for water took me to places of exquisite beauty. My mother had grown up on the coast of Maine. She vacationed every summer at her grandmother's cottage on Sandy Point. When she married, she moved inland to upstate New York, a whole day's trip from salt air. Every summer our family went east, to the water. We covered the northeastern coast of the United States and Canada. We camped around the Gaspé Peninsula in Canada and on the beaches of Prince Edward Island, Cape Breton, and Nova Scotia. We boated up and down the St. Lawrence River and island-hopped among the Thousand Islands. These pilgrimages to water every summer were more than restitution between my parents. It was water that filled my mother's soul.

I caught her passion. Water has the power to dissolve my petty preoccupations. It pulls me out of my small self and shows me the size of my soul self. When in water, on water, or next to water, I feel the lightness and calm that come after lovemaking. I love to swim in it, wash in it. Water holds the spirit of a place: Cayuga Lake, Lake Champlain, Caspian Lake. Water has great healing power. Now my four-year-old daughter is catching it. She has asked me, "Mommy, why do you love showers so much?" She can frolic in the pool all afternoon, can bathe for an hour and shower until the hot water runs out.

Last summer I indulged my daughter's passion for horses and took her to the childhood homestead and farm of a high school classmate. Over the years, the farm had become highly specialized for a very important purpose. My classmate's mother, Mrs. Alexander, now a grandmother of many, was the proud owner of a barn full of purebred Shetland ponies. Despite their tremendous value, they were not for sale. They were for loan only.

Ten years ago, a visitor had brought his young son to the farm to see the ponies. This child was special. He could not walk, talk, or move his arms or legs with any control. His body was bound by the reflexes and spasticity of cerebral palsy. "He was a bright little boy," said Mrs. Alexander. "You could see it in his eyes."

The boy was laid over the back of a pony. The boy grabbed the pony's mane with his hands. He lay on the horse's back for probably forty-five minutes. The horse stood perfectly still. The boy was in heaven, an experience of pure joy. When it was time to leave, the boy became very upset and cried the saddest tears.

It was this incident that set Mrs. Alexander afire and sent

her to the Shetland Islands, across the United States and Canada. "I could see the bond between this child and the pony . . . These children have so little opportunity to bond with anything in this world. So I decided my Shetlands were for them." Mrs. Alexander started a foundation, called Personal Ponies Limited, Inc.[1] The ponies are loaned, free, to children with physical handicaps only. "The Shetland pony is perfect for these children. They are unconditional in their acceptance. The children feel that. The Shetlands are ever patient, extremely gentle, and highly intelligent animals. Children can bond to them easily." They are also disease free, eat very little, and only need a backyard for exercise. They can live in suburbia.

When Mrs. Alexander is contacted by a family, she delivers the horse herself anywhere in the United States or Canada. She stays with the loan family for about four days. The family can keep the horse for as long as they want. The only condition is that there must be another animal or pet in the household. Mrs. Alexander explained, "It is extremely important for the pony to have another animal around for bonding."

There is a paradox to Mrs. Alexander's passion. "I myself have no patience for physical limitation," she said. "I am a Suzuki violin teacher; I brought the Suzuki method into this country. I am repulsed by physical handicaps and have no idea how to deal with them. But I know bonding when I see it. I can do this."

Mrs. Alexander is one of those people who lives beyond herself. She does not live self-consciously. As the mother of five children, she was visible in our public school. She was a beautiful woman with thick, long, dark hair and large snappy brown eyes. You knew her passion then.

Now her long hair is gone, her youthful beauty transformed into a fire, a passion for service, the kind of beauty that you see with your heart. Her heart has opened beyond her own children to ones she does not yet know or has not ever met.

Mrs. Alexander combined her greatest strength of nurturing and bonding with her self-admitted weakness, a repulsion for physical limitation. The mixture ignited a chemical reaction that bonded together her show-horse Shetlands and children with bound bodies.

Passion and Intimacy

Passion creates intimacy. Sharing a passion with another creates a bond that goes beyond the usual surface roles and personas. Just as our children know us best by our passions, so does everyone else. You don't really know someone until you know his or her passions. If you don't have any passions, then you don't really know yourself. When you decide to share your passion with another, you have made a decision about that relationship. You have made a decision to risk trust, and you have made a decision to move toward intimacy.

As I said before, most men seem to bond best around sports. They play the ball games (basketball, baseball, football); they golf, fish, bowl, boat, hunt, ski, and rock climb together.

Kate, the mother of two young sons, told me that she is pushing sports with her sons. One is naturally talented, but the other has to work at it. "It will give them a positive focus, give them a way to connect socially with others, and keep their bodies in shape so they can feel good about their appearance and feel attractive to the opposite sex when that becomes paramount. It will keep them in the right crowd of kids." Kate is not pushing her kids to excel, to be jocks, or to get athletic scholarships. She wants to provide them with access, a way to connect with their peers in a healthful way.

There is life beyond sports, even for men. Our friend Jeff loves opera. This is a passion he shares with his closest friend and colleague. I do not know if the friendship was formed by route of opera or medicine. I do know that these guys escape with their wives to the big cities several times a year for fine dining and opera. These couples do not have to work at finding their common ground, to try to think of ways to connect, or of things to do together. A shared passion makes intimacy easy.

I am not certain I would ever have connected with my husband if I had not had a rendezvous with Bob Dylan. Just prior to meeting my future husband, I was seeing a man who drenched me with Dylan. After dinner, it was our ritual to have some wine in the living room and listen to Dylan. I always wanted to listen to *Blood on the Tracks*. I'll admit, Dylan got under my skin. So for my birthday, my boyfriend gave me my very own album. When Dick, my future husband, was visiting at my apartment for the first time, he saw it, *Blood on the Tracks* sitting on the top of the turntable. He looked up at me and asked, "You like Dylan?" Without knowing the full significance of my response, I answered, "Yes." My husband's eyes lit up. We put on the album and danced. It was the beginning of us.

Years ago I attended a state conference on occupational therapy in hopes of networking with therapists who were working in the area of healing and well-being. I knew my agenda, and I tuned my sensors accordingly. At one workshop on gestalt therapy, I coincidentally ended up with a kindred spirit. She and I had to pair up for an exercise. We were the only ones left without partners, even though I was in the back row and she was in the front row. (There are no coincidences.) We hit it off. At the luncheon we were seated at a round table for eight, but there might as well have been just the two of us. We were totally engrossed in discovering each other. Each layer got better and better. I *finally* had met someone, the first person since my move of two years before, who spoke my language, who shared my passion. Today, Diane is a dear friend.

In *Secrets of a Very Good Marriage: Lessons from the Sea*, the author, Sherry Suib Cohen, finds herself on a fishing boat many more hours and days than she could ever have imagined. Fishing is her husband's passion. "Larry is always the second guy at the boatyard in March and sadly concedes defeat sometime after Thanksgiving." Fishing is her husband's renewal season and her "qualmish" season.[2] Cohen says, "Passion is not about romantic love, or orgiastic bliss from my groin to my imagination, it is taking a Coast Guard boat-maintenance course, so he appreciates your commitment to his obsession, he falls head over heels in love with you all over again."[3]

If we live with passion, we can learn by osmosis. Then learning is easy, a joy. Passion will take us places we would otherwise have no purpose in being, and it can create bonds and intimacy with others we would otherwise not know. If we live with passion, so will our children. Living with passion is being wholly alive.

15

RITUAL

First Comes Rhythm, Then Routine

THERE IS A rhythm to life. When life is new, there is a strong inner rhythm: sleep, eat, and wake. When the parent is able to read and respond to the inner rhythms of a child, life is peaceful, almost sublime. Gradually, the inner rhythm of the child adjusts to the outer rhythms of the world. The inner rhythms are still in play, but as the child awakens more and more to the world, routine becomes the organizing element in a child's life. It is routine that bridges the adult and child worlds. Children love routine. It is their security blanket. Routine is the secret survival strategy for anyone who cares for children—parents, teachers, or child-care providers. It is routine that creates order first in the environment and then within the child.

Routine gives shape and form to the wide-open space of

a day for the very young child and to the week for the older child. Without routine, a child's energy is wheeling. It is routine that routes a child's energy into a given place, with given people, with a given plan. It is within the boundaries of routine that children feel enveloped and embraced; they know they have a place. It gives them an internal sense of belonging. They can relax. They do not have to anxiously look around the landscape in search of an attachment.

Then there comes a time when routine needs to be broken with change. If we have too much routine, life starts to feel bland. From time to time, life needs to be opened up and filled out with new sights, smells, sounds, sensations. We need Halloween, birthdays, Valentine's Day, July Fourth, and Thanksgiving.

These special occasions are adopted by our children, eventually. They are anticipated with great excitement, eventually. Every parent can appreciate the humor of the first birthday, the first Christmas. We make elaborate preparations, and pomp to boot, all to the bewilderment of our precious little ones. It takes at least two go-arounds before our children catch onto these once-a-year rituals.

The Love of Ritual

Children need ritual long before their first birthdays. Children love ritual. They thrive on ritual and are great ritual makers. Babies let us know very early if their wakeful time is in the a.m. or p.m. (the morning versus night person), if they like tight covers or no covers, if they like to be walked or rocked, or if they are marathoners or cat-nappers. Of course, some of these personal rituals change, but some remain the same. Some are learned; some seem intrinsic, if not genetic. When I was first married, I thought it curious the way my husband always tucked in the sheet and blanket at the end of the bed before getting into the already-made bed. "How long have you been doing that?" I asked. "Forever," he said.

Later, as children become more socialized, they ritualize play. Their squeals of joy are so delicious that we play along and will even make fools of ourselves in public: "Soooo big," "patty cake, patty cake," "peek-a-boo." Then within the year come "Twinkle, Twinkle, Little Star" and "This Little Light of Mine" and "The Itsy Bitsy Spider." All parents can name at least one book that they have read to their child at least fifty times, such as *Goodnight Moon, Brown Bear, Brown Bear, What Do You See?* and *Love You Forever.* It is the repetition and anticipation that create ritual. In the song or book, it is the rhythm, rhyme, and repetition that bring such delight. The same can be said for our personal rituals, our routines, and our annual and seasonal rituals or holidays.

The Power of the Three R's

Rhythm, routine, and ritual all work in rotation. We all feel our best, work our best, and live our best when we honor our rhythms, routines, and rituals. To ignore our need for the three basic R's of life in their proper rotation is to live life like a run-on sentence with no punctuation. Our lives lack cadence and style. When our lives just run on, we sometimes don't even know what we need most, routine or ritual, the icing or the cake.

Children will rip wide open our established rhythms, routines, and rituals. To re-establish our equilibrium and sense of homeostasis takes tremendous work, ingenuity, and sometimes just sheer grit: "I *will* have my shower today!" It takes years to re-establish the three R's in our new life, both as a whole person and as a whole family. And to complicate things, life is always in flux, always changing.

I have come to appreciate that rhythm, routine, and ritual are my most powerful tools as a parent. Appreciation comes with repetition. It is knowing my rhythms and those of the members of my family that allows me to create an environment of harmony and peace at best and divert crisis and disaster at the very least. It is the deliberate use of routine that conserves everyone's precious energy. The maintenance part of life is on automatic pilot so that everyone can do the more important business of their lives: playing, learning, and creating. It is the creation and use of ritual that highlights the gifts of life, bringing them to the forefront to be acknowledged, honored, and celebrated. It is the repetition of created and traditional family rituals that makes my children feel intimately connected to their own family and to the world at large. It is through the three R's that my children have a stabilizing sense of continuity, control, and order, even when change is all around them and within them. It is when my children drop a ritual that I know they have grown, and I know that when they return to a ritual they need an extra dose of comfort or security. We never grow out of our need for ritual, nor should we. Growing up is learning the importance and power of the three basic R's of life. It is the three R's that are the foundation for homeostasis and wholeness.

Family Rituals

My husband and I once asked Ed, our senior friend and seasoned father of three happy and prospering grown children, what the secret was to his successful parenting. Chuckling, he said, "My wife and their mother." We still pressed him. We wanted a father's perspective. His family was close, even with his children dispersed, out of the nest. After a moment of reflection, he said, "Family rituals." We asked him to specify. "It doesn't matter what they are," he said, "as long as you have them."

When I was growing up, we celebrated all the traditional holidays. They were special times, a pause in everyday life. But it was the family rituals within the cultural traditions that gave the holidays our family signature: the lobster Newburg Christmas Eve supper, the birthday presents in the morning and cake at night, and the colored egg tree at Easter. Off-season family rituals were just as dear, if not more so.

My mother and I always had a ritual of going up on Snyder Hill to pick May flowers, or arbutus as we called them. Arbutus blooms early in the spring; the flowers grow as ground cover and have to be hunted for very carefully. Because they are rare, we each picked just enough for a small teacup bouquet, one for her room and one for mine. Arbutus had the most fragile smell. A teacupful could scent a bedroom for only a day, and then they were gone. Some years we didn't time it right, and they were already past, dried up under the ground pine.

When my family traveled to the coast of Maine, we would always get lobster, not in a fancy restaurant but at the lobster pound out on the pier, and then take our baskets out by the water and crack the shells open on the rocks. Whenever we visit my husband's family, my mother-in-law always serves salmon with cream cheese and bagels for breakfast. One of my children's favorite rituals is Friday night at Friday's, the restaurant. We digest our week over dinner and plan out our weekend together.

In her book *New Traditions*, Susan Abel Lieberman warns, "Don't procrastinate . . . Time has a way of surprising us with its cumulative speed. For years, it seemed we would never move beyond diapers and Dr. Seuss. Now I want to catch hold of time." [Her sons are eleven and nine.] Within the decade both boys will be off to college . . . This period of time when the children are old enough to be a real part of our family activities, to contribute to them and enjoy them and yet still be young enough to like cuddling and giggling with their parents, suddenly seems so short. It also seems so busy. If we don't pay attention, it slips away from us before we have established the kinds of ties that bond us together as distance and time pull us apart."[1]

Creating Community Through Ritual

Most neighborhoods today are quiet from eight to five, Monday through Friday, and weekends are also spoken for, with special lessons, sports, club activities, and necessary household maintenance. If we are to ever know our neighbors, the people who live right next to us, we will have to block out some time, put "neighborhood" on the calendar. In my new neighborhood, we put the block idea to good use. The weekend after Labor Day, the entire street of four blocks is closed to traffic. Everyone is out on roller blades, bikes, trikes, wagons, strollers, or just in plain old Nikes. We picnic in the street. At dusk, the day is topped off with sparklers for the kids. A former neighbor always ended the summer with a corn roast in the backyard. During the dark days of winter, neighbors keep in touch with soup and salad suppers and progressive dinners.

Creating Ritual

Annual Award Ceremony

Sometimes it is out of necessity, maybe even desperation, that the best traditions get created. I never liked New Year's Eve. I do not remember one party or celebration that I can remember enjoying. I guess I thought, "What is so great about ending a year, unless it was particularly bad?" As for children, they do not really grasp the concept of "year" until they are writing the date on their school papers. So instead of just passing by another year, I created The Aronson Annual Award Ceremony. My husband and I make up about ten awards for each member of the family. The category is written on the outside of the envelope. On the inside is the gold paper medallion with the winner's name on the back. This is the way our family reviews the year together, the events, joys, funnies, successes, and accomplishments that punctuated that particular year. Everyone guesses whom the award will go to; there is lots of hooting and howling. Just for fun, we sometimes stick in other people. This year's "best body" went to Eric, Toby's swim instructor.

Family rituals need not take weeks to plan and days to execute. Our New Year's Day award ceremony takes about one hour to create. Lieberman tells how one of her children's most cherished traditions is waking to find "Happy Birthday" written on the bathroom mirror in toothpaste, "a one-minute ritual born years ago when I couldn't find the silver banner and was too tired to make a sign."[2]

Ritual of Welcome

On the eve of the birth of my second child, I was preoccupied. Yes, the birth and all that—but also about the social support in place for my family. We had moved halfway across the country within the year. Our social network was young and small. Extended family was over one thousand miles away. I wanted my son to be supported and recognized for becoming a brother, and I wanted someone there to be with him while his parents labored at the hospital. I wanted a community of people to welcome our newborn into the world, to give their blessings.

I decided what I needed was a "Ritual of Welcome," which is deeply rooted in human experience. So I set it up, schedule and all. I asked six families we knew to become members of our birth support team. Even though the members of our family support team had not been close friends, they responded as if they were. They had been invited to partake in an intimate part of our family life. One member took care of our son on the birth night; others brought meals and gifts to honor a new brother. They whispered words of welcome to our newborn, listened to the birth story, and shared our joy.

HouseWrap

Now we are living in a new home. We are eager to get acquainted with our neighbors and build community. We don't know how long we will be here, in this home, in this neighborhood. We can choose to just get acquainted over the years, or we can be a catalyst for creating community deliberately. Just as Lieberman said, "Don't procrastinate with family ritual building," the same applies to neighborhood building. So we had a HouseWrap, otherwise known as a housewarming or house blessing. We told our friends it was a New England tradition. To begin, guests signed our book by putting down some personal thoughts on the meaning of home. We then read their words in assembly and literally wrapped the house in three colors of crepe paper: pink for health, yellow for happiness, and purple for prosperity. At the end, we 'fessed up and told our guests the truth, "We made it up." "Ohhh," they all groaned in unison. A surge of spontaneous cheers and applause followed. "We want our house wrapped too!"

This is what one person wrote in our HouseWrap book: "Home is the expression of your collective spirits. May your souls evolve as you fill it with your love, experiences, and, yes, rituals."

Part III

Growing Whole

16

ON HOMEBASE

Feeling Like Myself

WE COULD NOT hold out any longer. We had to tell Toby our decision. We were sitting in the parking lot about to embark on our Sunday afternoon bike ride by the lake. In the car, he had asked us repeatedly if we were going to move. We were trying to spare ourselves the drama, the fallout, the grief. And did we ever get it, full force, a total eruption. It was volcanic, fireworks in all directions. "I hate you! No! I won't go! I hate Greenfield!" He cried raw tears. As parents, we felt shredded. Toby would not let us comfort him; he pushed us away and out of our arms. He knew he had no power in reversing our decision. But he had power over himself, and he refused to let us interrupt, usurp, squelch, or suppress his total and complete expression of pain, his experience with loss and grief. Amongst all the debris that he was throwing at us came his truth: "I don't want to move; this is where I feel like myself." My son had fused our house, the dwelling, with safety, being able to be himself, where he felt most comfortable in the world. In his mind, it was the specific location, that quarter-acre plot in the universe where he could be all of himself.

So, home is where you feel like yourself, your whole self. It is where you can share the outer edges of feelings and thoughts in safety. As our friend and neighbor Mary Shapiro wrote in our housewarming book, "Home is where you kick off your shoes, graze in the fridge, leave cups and glasses around, and talk about what's going on (outside) with people who care about you most (those inside)."

It was understandable; our son had lived at 29 Sycamore Street for six out of his eight years. For him, it was not just a home, but his only home. But my husband and I knew better. We had each experienced "home" in a number of different places. We had each experienced strong community. Paradoxically, the reason for our decision to move was to live where we could feel more like ourselves. We wanted to love where we lived, to embrace it, to put down roots, to move out of our suburban ambivalence that kept us living on the outskirts of our more genuine selves. So we moved in, closer to the center of the city and closer to where "I feel like myself."

As parents, we knew what made our son "feel like himself" would not be lost or left behind. What made him feel like himself were the rhythms, tone, idiosyncrasies, habits, rituals, values, life-style, signature, spirit, and love of his particular and sometimes peculiar family. So how do you make "home" in the world? If it is not a place, a dwelling, then what is it?

Belonging

Home is where you belong. We tend to think of belonging in terms of time. The longer we are somewhere or with someone, the greater the sense of belonging. Our first belongings are made for us: the family we are born into, the community we grow up in, the religion we practice, the school we attend, and perhaps even our first friends. We need to start somewhere. I believe that the content is not as important as the context. It is more important to feel that sense of belonging, to know that we are meant to be affiliated and connected, so that we will not settle for less. That knowing will be our children's protection, their security. They will not settle for less.

When my nephew was eight, he asked his parents, "What am I?" As you can imagine, his parents were bewildered by their son's question. What could he mean? Boy, white, Anglo-Saxon, middle class, Democrat? "What do you mean? Can you be more specific about what you are thinking about?" his parents asked. "Sure . . . Am I a Catholic, Methodist, Baptist, Presbyterian, or what?" asked my nephew. This was right on cue. At about age eight or nine, children want an identification with a religion; it is part of the package of individuation and self-identity.

Many of us baby-boomer parents have rejected the religion, or more specifically the religious indoctrination, of our youth. We saw through the institution and hypocrisies of the church. We don't want to subject our children to it. But it did give us an identity, a belonging, even if we chose to reject it as adults. We even say, I am a Catholic or a Jew, however non-practicing we might be.

At Least One Place

The long-anticipated event was now over. My neighbor Ruth looked tired but tranquil. "Ah, it was really very moving," she said. "I got so caught up in the planning and arrangements that it wasn't until I was sitting there during the bar mitzvah did it really hit me what this was all about."

For Daniel's mother, the bar mitzvah was not just about

becoming. It was about belonging. It was the ritual and witness of her son passing into adulthood before a community of people to which he now belonged in his own right. She almost seemed relieved, as if her load as a parent had been lightened. "Wherever he goes, he knows at least one place he belongs; it can be a kind of anchor for him. Jim [her husband] and I won't be here forever; he needs to know where he belongs ... This way he won't spend his whole life searching ... "

In adulthood, we must make our own decisions to belong or not belong to affiliations made in childhood. Americans are movers. Our realtor told us that the average stay in a home is just five years. Staying in one place, be-looonging, is not possible for most of us. We need other ways to belong that are not dependent on time. Many use their professions; others use religious affiliation, community service, or sports and recreation as ways to connect in new places.

Belonging is not just a matter of living or working somewhere. Belonging is a decision. A close friend from Vermont once told me, "You belong when you decide that you do." It is deciding to be a player on the field of life and being open for the passes that come your way. It is digging deeply into life, putting down roots so you can grow and bear fruit. If we sow on the surface, we feel blown away with every changing wind.

Homesick

It is hard to admit we are homesick. It makes us feel like children. My mother once said, "All three of you kids got homesick when you went away to college. You were really sick—you ran fevers and suffered from malaise, aches, and chills just like a flu." It is the sickness of not yet belonging to any person(s) nor feeling an association or attachment to any place(s) in your new home. It is the sickness of separation from the old and the sickness of not yet being connected to the new. Transitions can make you homesick.

I knew a woman who came to our city—which has a low crime rate and is affordable and beautiful—to take a challenging job at the university in nutrition research, a real catch, an excellent career opportunity. But every time I saw Karen, she was sick with one physical ailment after another and very negative about our midwestern city of "bikes, brats, and beer." (Karen was raised on the theater, museums, and real ethnic food.) She always looked exhausted and pale. She was homesick. In time, she was bitter about her job too. It was the only thing that held her here. If she made that bad too, she was free to go. Within three years, Karen made her break. She went back to New York and took a job at the United Nations, where she is in charge of a world hunger relief program. World hunger was her passion, something she could not pursue in academia. Last I heard, she was thriving. She was back home.

Home is wherever your pulse beats strong and steady. It is wherever you are open, where the valves between your inner and outer worlds are open and circulating—the inner world that feeds the soul and the outer world that lives your purpose. It is like the air heating system in a house. If there are not enough return vents, the air does not circulate. The air becomes stale. The soul wilts. If there are not enough out vents, the room never heats up; there is not enough fire in the soul.

Staying in Yourself

One Saturday morning in early spring, when the sun rose at five, our family was all cuddled in bed so Dad and Mom could sleep an hour or so longer. "Mom, my allergies are back." I tried to sound interested, but sleep was hanging heavy over my body. I managed a halfhearted "uh-huh." "Mom! I almost fell asleep in Reach class yesterday and again riding home on the bus. The kid sitting next to me had to wake me up at our stop." "Ohhh?" I turned over and opened half an eye at him. I was concerned, but later, later. He persisted, "Mommmm, when I was writing, I tried to think of how to spell 'twist,' and it took me ten seconds to think of the letter 'T.' It feels like my brain is moving in slow motion. I wish I had someone else's body." It worked. I sat up. My four-year-old daughter, who was listening to all of this from the master bath, returned to the bedroom with her finger pointing at my son, who was lying in bed. With a Wicked-Witch-of-the-West look, she said, "Now, you stay in yourself." We all roared.

Some people seem to stay in themselves, no matter where they are. Val was such a woman. We met on "The Farm," a cross-country ski resort in central Wisconsin. She lived in Illinois, just over the southern Wisconsin border. Val was from North Carolina. She had been in Illinois just over a year. She was a comic and entertained us well at dinner. My stomach ached from laughter as she caricatured the outgoing and friendly southerner (I too had lived in North Carolina) and the small town midwesterner, whom she affectionately called "personality free." Her new midwestern friends and neighbors were more reserved than what Val was accustomed to in the South. "They stayed close to the chest," said Val. One of Val's stories was about her first Parent-Teacher Organization (PTO) meeting at her sons' new school. "I was quite vocal, but I got the feeling my opinions were not always welcomed." The response was an embarrassed silence. The next day she got a call from the principal with an invitation to start a volunteer tutoring program at the school. She stayed in herself and made home in one night.

Community

Several years ago I invited my friend Cindy, a psychologist, to a seminar on family and self-esteem. The speaker focused on the "tapes," or self-talk, that children hear in their heads and play out in their lives. The messages on these tapes are recorded by parents, teachers, and other important adults in a child's life. The speaker was suggesting that our self-esteem is an inner phenomenon that can be changed for the better by redoing our inner "tapes."

As the speaker lectured to the ballroom-sized audience, I could feel my friend bristle beside me. Afterwards we talked about it on the way home in the car. It was a hot, humid summer night. The air was heavy in the car; there was no air conditioning in my twelve-year-old Volvo. "So what did you think?" Cindy asked. (Psychologists love open-ended questions.) I'm more judgmental. I jumped right in. "I was disappointed; it was pretty basic, nothing I haven't heard before." Knowing that she would not offend me, she shared her own opinion. "Self-esteem does not happen in a social vacuum. You cannot talk your way into or out of esteem. Self-esteem is from being a valued member of a group, be it a family, community, or society. That is why people are suffering from a lack of self-esteem. Because we are all disconnected from one another . . . "

Renowned physician Rachel Naomi Remen has spent her career in medicine trying to understand the mystery of healing. She has come to believe that "healing is generally a work of relationship, that ordinary people heal one another."[1] Community is a powerful antidote for dis-ease. Unless we live in community, where our inner and outer lives can circulate, we will be "homesick" whether we know it or not.

Home Is Not Far Away

Natalie, my friend from high school, never left home, but she was homesick. She has lived all of her life (except for college) within a twenty-mile radius. Of all my high school friends, she is the one that I would have most expected to leave the area. In high school, she complained about small-town life. She hungered for a bigger world, more urban, with greater culture, a vibrancy that comes from cities, not from rural America. She loved art; she was starving for it. She wanted to immerse herself in it. In college she was nurtured as an artist, and she blossomed. But she ended up back home again. She took jobs teaching art at local high schools. Again, she complained bitterly about the schools' conservatism. She was thrashing; she felt boxed in, but she could not find her way out. Her body was finding a way out. It was taking charge. She became very sick.

Something had to change. Her body said, "No more. You need to find your way home." During the relief of summer break, and when she was recovered in body and no doubt changed in soul, it happened. On a chance, last-minute invitation to a potluck supper at a friend's, Natalie met a man with whom she could share her passion for art, for culture, for a different world view; he found a woman who embraced her femininity, was progressive in her thinking and politics, and who was a talented artist. It was a match. Through her husband-to-be, Natalie entered a completely different world just twenty miles from where she had grown up. Through this relationship, she was able to move into her whole self at last. She is now a prolific artist. When she became a mother, she was torn between her art and parenting. She knew she needed her art to stay alive. So like all the rest of us, Natalie is searching for balance. Last time I spoke with her, she said, "You'll never guess what I'm doing. I'm teaching art in Katie's [her daughter] school two mornings a week ... I just love it, the kids are just so enthusiastic!" She is building an ever wider community; she is circulating. She is home.

To be at home, we need to keep our inner and outer worlds circulating. Actually, I think my friend Susan had it right. After giving birth to her second child, she was feeling some need for change. She said, "I am losing weight through aerobics, I got my hair restyled and colored, I am starting a reading group in the neighborhood, and I am enrolling in an interior design class. I am doing an overhaul, both the inside and outside. I've come to the conclusion that you've got to do both, the inside and the outside."

Yes, home is where we feel ourselves, where we belong, where we can circulate our inner and outer worlds, where we can build an ever expanding and changing community. But home at its root is love. When we are home, we can love the fullest; we like ourselves and let others like us. We grow on the inside and on the outside. We feel right; we feel home.

When I look for home in my own life, I still think of places, special places, places where love was born, blossomed, or grew and circulated around in my life: 125 West Main Street, Hill Hall, 9 Marian Street, Highland Lodge, Weston Priory, Owen Park, Picnic Point, Searsport, Cayuga Lake State Park, Red Rocks . . .

We can teach our children how to make home by how we live. We need to find a place to belong, embrace it, and put down roots. A home needs a strong foundation to survive the rocking thunder of celebration and the turbulence of storms. Community is the foundation for health and home, so we can "feel like ourselves."

17

SEXY SPIRIT

Sex A.D. (After Diapers)

IT WAS MOM'S night out. We were all suffering from cabin fever at winter's end. No sun for weeks—just wet, gray, and cold. Someone suggested we spice up our dinner conversation by sharing sex secrets. "Where was the most unusual place you had sex?" suggested one mom. "And not necessarily with your husband," she added. "At the beach; the laundromat; on the pool table?"

Those were the days, B.C., before children.

Brenda, the mother of three children under three, said her husband wanted to know when they would be having sex again. Another mother of two preschoolers said her husband wished they were back in their courtship. Susannah said the passion was gone from her marriage. It was practically unanimous: sex after children had lost its lust; the allure had faded. So what happened? When we dropped our babies, we did not drop our beauty. These moms knew how to look good. We fit into designer jeans; no one needed to cover up with oversized sweaters. We were finished off with skinny belts, earrings, and eye makeup.

For starters, introduce sleep deprivation, exhaustion, and raging hormones. You begin to wonder what you ever saw in sex. Your libido is flat on its back. In the words of renowned pediatrician and mother Penelope Leach, " . . . you are so tired you don't want dinner or sex; the only thing in the world you want is to go to sleep."[1] "Not tonight, honey" stretches into a month and longer . . .

Sometime after the fatigue fog has lifted, an average of six months, you and your mate wake up to a whole new reality. The time you and your mate reserved for one another has vanished. No more lingering and languorous time in bed on weekends or quickies on weekday mornings. The spontaneous weekend getaways you packaged together on Friday afternoons look far in the distance now. Even the simple things, such as an involved conversation or a hand-holding stroll around the neighborhood, seem like luxuries. You feel lucky if you can get out for a movie or meal together, if you can find a baby-sitter.

It is not long before the power struggles begin, over who gets time out and who watches the kids. The personal time that was once used for being with one another gets divided between both parents to get a break. A physician friend equated it to residency. "Once you have kids," she said, "you are always on call. Just to run to the corner store or take a shower in peace, you've got to be covered by your other half."

You feel as if you are sliding down the slippery slope of Maslow's hierarchy of needs. A real descent. You feel indignant at nature's dirty trick. There you were, self-actualization within your reach, on the crest of your career; finances were stable and life was good, so you decided to start a family and share your good fortune. Now here you are, regressed to the survival mode. The laundry is piling up, the grocery bags sit on the countertops, and you haven't brushed your teeth yet today. Not a very sexy scene.

You soon learn that parenting is developmental. Just as you get a handle on one stage, you're on to the next. Just when you have conquered chronic fatigue and chaos, in comes constant interruption. This is the time when the child's mouth and motor are in full gear. It plays real havoc with husband-and-wife communication. "Mom," "Mom!" "Mommm!!" Barbara, mother of three, thought she was losing it when she came down with the "dizzies," an ailment caused by rapid head turning. It's a real challenge to get a word in or around the edges with one's spouse, let alone anything heart to heart. Communication has been reduced to sound bites: "We need milk; the phone; where are the keys?" This is neither flattering to our intelligence nor enriching to our love.

It is hard to unleash your passion onto your mate when you have no privacy. So you miss those afternoon frolics on the weekends? Well, there is always nap time. Forget it, we already tried that. Children have a sixth sense that they are missing the fun and wake up just when the juices get flowing. To get lovemaking in before the day begins, you'll have to set the alarm for five. No one looks good at that hour. That leaves after bedtime. Many parents I know are so tired at the end of the day that their children are running circles around them. You use the last ounces of energy you have left to get them down. If getting the pajamas on doesn't do you in, the toothbrushing will. This is the time children pay you back for any transgression you have committed against them during the day. You fall into a heap on your own bed, sacked out. At this point, the closest you'll get to sex is to sink your weight into your mate's as you snooze, belly on belly.

Warning: We all know couples who work well together as

domestic partners and share responsibilities of family support and child-rearing but lack spirit in their relationship. We cannot imagine that their sex life is active. Husband and wife insidiously become Mom and Dad and domestic business partners. Cringe. Some never recover. You can see them out for supper after the children are grown, eating without exchanging more than a couple of sound bites, probably about the food.

Put it all together and it is *a hotbed for a major sex cool.*

Barrier-Free Relief

There seem to be so many barriers to having fulfilling sex after children. The structures we created with our mates for intimacy are gone. For me and my husband, it was the Saturday morning walk downtown, the Sunday afternoon nap, the picnic during lunch hour, or our favorite country inn. These were the rituals we created to stay close and connected. After baby, they took their places on the mantel of our memories that we stop to look at longingly from time to time. We console ourselves by thinking we'll get back there again someday...

There is no point in waiting for the time when our lives are freed up. It will never come, or no one will be there when we are. The challenge is to create new structures for loving sex beyond our own sagging beds—something that fits our new life-style, our new rhythm. Children need not obliterate or stifle our sex lives. They simply present us with a challenge.

To have fulfilling sex, you need to be turned on. You cannot just undress, jump into an unmade bed at the end of the day, and expect fireworks; it just doesn't work that way. You have to court sex. It is all in the foreplay. It is foreplay that makes great sex. Foreplay can happen anywhere, anytime. You don't even have to be in the same room. That's great news for parents. Foreplay is barrier free, and that includes children. (Foreplay spells: *for* *e*xpanding *p*arent's *l*ongings *a*nd *y*earnings.)

Foreplay can be a look, a touch, a scent, a word. My husband and I foreplay best on the phone. Actually, it was through my husband's voice that I fell in love with the rest of him. Because of distance, we courted over the phone. Still today, it is his voice that arouses me most. It is deep, compassionate, sensual, and sexual. When we talk on the phone, he is all there, never reviewing a report or typing at his computer at the same time. He will never get a car phone; he never uses the cordless phone. Just as he speaks deeply, he listens deeply. He is generous. Sometimes I have lots to say.

Foreplay is the spirit at work in any intimate relationship. Spirit is magnetic, extremely attractive, and downright sexy. It was the spirit of your mate that attracted you in the first place. When we are full of spirit, we are turned on and are a turn-on to others. We shine; we are at our best. We like to be around people who are exercising their spirit. It is energizing; it is fun; it lightens us up. When someone focuses spirit on us, it is a rush. We fall into love, if only for a moment.

It is foreplay that provides the running current or charge in a marriage. Making love becomes ongoing, open-ended, and endless. No longer is it the Saturday night, after-the-movie routine. Making love is no longer bound to the bed. It is our dear children who force us to break free of this limited version of lovemaking and catapult onto a much larger playing field.

So what does a running (fore)play look like?

Borrow some ideas from your favorite sport, such as football. Call to your mate in audibles, like a quarterback does to change a play, a language you can speak in front of the kids. Rush with sustained eye contact. Press hard with deep hugs. Plan a blitz. Share your shining moments, your successes and inspirations, when they are still fresh. Contact each other when the excitement is still in your voice.

Give your mate your best shot: go to a professional photographer and get framed so your mate can take the "magnificent you" to work and carry you around in purse or pocket.

Show your mate you know him better than anyone else. Record his favorite love songs or the soundtrack of a favorite movie on a cassette for the car tape deck. Entitle it "Passionately Yours."

Compliment your mate aloud, especially in public. No put-downs, ever. Only lift-ups.

Honor your mate by the way you dress, scent, and speak.

Invite your mate to share your passions, be they opera, gardening, skiing, or softball, so your mate can see your spirit in full bloom.

Give your mate some prime time. Meet for lunch at your favorite spot, or check out of work and into a hotel for the afternoon.

Set aside sacred time to spend with your mate each week. Lock in a baby-sitter for that time.

Try to spend time with people who reflect back to you your beauty and appreciate and honor your spirit. Avoid those who do not.

Foreplay is the saving grace to the sagging sex saga of parents. It serves as a kind of culture for the continuous breeding of love. This is powerful stuff. It can lead to creation itself.

The Marriage of Sex and Spirit

It is the making of our children, in flesh and blood, that join sex and spirit in the first place. During conception and childbirth we experience the true ecstasy of sex and spirit beyond sensual pleasure, passion, or orgasm. These are just hints of the shattering explosion of love from and into the universe that we experience with the coming of children.

In conscious conception, a couple invites a soul to come forth and be embraced into the fold of their lovemaking. It is love that draws the incoming soul. Likes attract likes. The greater the love exchange between the couple, the more delicacy the soul has to work with in creating its form. As the couple makes love, they float weightless in the womb of creation. They are timeless; there is no before or after. There is only All.

The euphoria of childbirth is a feeling of connection to all people and all time. Childbirth is a peak experience. For a woman, it is the time she fully realizes the power of her body and the ageless memory in her body's cells to do the work of delivering her babe into the world. The power of her body can be frightening; she has to give in to it just as she gives in or lets go to receive during sex. It is during childbirth that a woman feels connected to all mothers who have come before her and all who shall come after her, all at the same time; it is overwhelming. We cry, we scream, we call out in ancient and primitive ways. There is fluid, sweat, blood everywhere. It is a holy mess. After I gave birth to my daughter, a very intense and rapid birth, my attending nurse came in and said she would promptly start to clean up the mess. I protested strongly. I wanted to lie in the holy waters of the womb.

Even though the father does not have the intense physical experience of birth, he can share the spiritual experience. Mark Gerzon, author of *Coming into Our Own: Understanding the Adult Metamorphosis*, describes his experience with birth this way: "Shelley and I gave birth to three sons . . . each time I was so moved by the spirit in the room that I felt the presence of a force greater than Shelley and me, greater certainly than sex, greater than our bodies, greater than human consciousness—something as great as the very force of Life itself."[2]

After we have our children, lovemaking is sustaining not only to us but to them as well. When parents make love it nourishes the child, a kind of vitamin L. Make love, make bread, make family, make heaven. Children know when their parents have made love. They like it; they know there will be more for them, just like bread. They do not consciously understand, but they sense a special something that they experience as joy. They take it in, not through their bodies but through their spirits. I can remember as a child my curiosity with certain mornings, when my parents spoke their pet names and moaned their hug in the kitchen. I could feel the new softness of my mother like the brushed fabric of her robe. The furrow in my father's brow was gone. That opened his sea-blue eyes. His lips were full. They seemed to be in another place, different from the usual workaday world and routine. I knew it was private, but it made me feel good, too.

Sex is the most delicate indicator of our state of being and the state of our intimate relationship. When we are without sex, we feel we have lost our spirit. When we are without spirit, we do not feel like having sex. Sex and spirit are symbiotic.

It is sex that gives us access to the soul. That is why we cry after we have made love, wholly love. We have touched the exquisite beauty of our soul. That is why we embrace our mate with our whole being after the consummation of our love. We have communed with the splendor of her/his soul.

It is sex that embodies the soul and brings it into the flesh. Sex is diving for the soul or soul diving. It is not enough to find it; it must be brought up to the surface and into the light so we can see it and become it. With it comes greater clarity of our purpose, our next step toward wholeness. We feel more peaceful and loving toward ourselves, our mate, our children, and life itself.

That is the ultimate purpose of marriage. Marriage is not about mating for sex; it is not about mating for children. It is about mating for soul. Soul-mating. Sex and children just lead us to it. We discover this revelation just when we think it is all over. The passion is gone; there is no charge, the Mom's-night-out syndrome. We feel stifled by the habits of living together. We feel flat. Our relationships feel flat. We feel this way because we have passed through the earlier chapters of marriage and we don't know where else to go; we may start looking "out there." We don't know there is more. No one ever told us because few have lived it; few know. There are many marriages that lack spirit, that have no soul. It may have nothing to do with children. But it is our children who give us a magnanimous reason to find it. It is time to mate our soul. It is time to marry our soulmate.

To get access to the soul through sex, you need a soulmate. You cannot dive deep without one. A soulmate is not found "out there" somewhere, if you could only find him or her; soulmates are not found in new love. A soulmate is created over years of loving and caring, forgiving the forgivable, and over years of trusting. A soulmate is rare. It is like land. We do not really know it until we have "walked it" in all seasons, all weathers, all lights, the dawn, the dusk, in the dark of night and in full sun. The picture is always new, always changing, even from the same spot. It is so much more than we thought when we first looked at it one day, in one season, in one light. We watch new growth take root, adding diversity and complexity to the landscape. We see that it is ever changing, full of life and full of soul.

To thrive, a marriage must find its soul. It takes spirit; it takes sex. They belong in the same bed. When looking for one, you find the other. Foreplay (spirit) gives us access to sex, and sex gives us access to our soul, the soul of our mate, and the soul of our marriage. A soulful marriage is the most valuable natural resource we can pass on to our children, more precious than premium land. Renowned American writer Madeleine L'Engle, soulmate to husband Hugh Franklin and mother of three, said that the best thing she and her husband did for their children was to love the other.[3] During the best of times, our children thrive on it and, at the very least, depend on it.

18

PEELING BACK THE BAND-AID®

FEW OF US make it to adulthood without some wounds. It is inevitable. We live in an imperfect world. More often than not, our wounds are unhealed. We don't even know we have them. In order to go on with our lives, we put on a Band-Aid.

Our wounds come from our relationships, our parents, siblings, friends, teachers, lovers, and bosses. Our wounds are the price of others' imperfections and our own perceptions and misperceptions. As adults, we have our wrinkles, and we have our wounds. And it is our responsibility to heal them. *For parents to finish the healing work of their lives is the ultimate act of loving and caring for their children.* If we don't, we burden our children with our unhealed wounds. They will take them on; they will carry our unhealed wounds into their own lives; they will adopt them by osmosis.

Sometimes it is crisis that peels back the Band-Aid, exposing our unhealed wounds; sometimes it is our struggle to grow more whole. Sometimes it is just life itself, and sometimes it is our children. As our children progress through development, the ghosts of our own childhood visit us.

You can be wounded at any age. So why focus on childhood? Childhood wounds cut deep; they go to the core. It is the most impressionable age. Children are the most vulnerable, tender, and open. Children are egocentric; they personalize everything. Whatever happens to them, they think they deserve. Childhood wounds are easily missed, outside of raw abuse and neglect. Childhood wounds can seem inconsequential, almost silly to the adult. It can take just one hurt to make a wound.

Childhood is when we made hard-to-change decisions about ourselves and about life. Children are like peaches— they bruise very easily. A seemingly minor childhood wound, if unhealed, grows just as the child does, so that when the child reaches adulthood the wound is adult-sized. What differentiates just another childhood experience from a wound is what decision a child makes about it. Decisions like: "I am clumsy, I cannot do math, I sing like a frog, feelings hurt you, I must be perfect," are wounds.

Children's decisions about themselves will bias further life experience in favor of their decisions. It will take a powerful experience(s) to the contrary to change their decisions, to heal their wounds.

The trouble with unhealed wounds is that they diminish your magnificence. A unhealed wound may keep you at arm's length from your gift—the special gift you were meant to share with the world, the one you were born with. An unhealed wound may siphon off energy so your power and light are diminished. You use your energy to protect it, like the post-surgical patient who walks crouched over, holding his guts together under folded arms. Unhealed wounds may be infected with greedy emotions like fear, anger, resentment, or jealousy. An unhealed wound may block the flow of your heart, your spirit, or your mind. It is safer to keep risk low, adventure tame, and thinking narrow.

Whistle Wound

Take whistling. It is pleasant enough, a nice skill. But whistling is not a requirement. Right? It is completely optional. If I remember correctly, my kindergarten teacher tried to teach us to whistle as part of a song during music time. She "tested" us one at a time around the circle as we sat on our respective mats. Since I was quite shy, this mortified me. When it came my turn, I could not do it—not a peep. I think I was the only one in the class who flunked whistling. "Oh, Linda has a frog in her throat," she sang. The kids laughed. This happened several days running. It seemed like weeks. My five-year-old self was embarrassed and ashamed.

Years later, whenever I had to speak in class or perform in front of an audience, I flipped into fear, the whole physiological mess, even though I had no memory at that time of my failed whistling debut. My sympathetic nervous system was working overtime: pounding heart, dry mouth, sweaty hands, shaking limbs, and hyperactive intestines. It is a wonder I ever tried. The only way I got through public speaking as an adult was to be over prepared and over rehearsed. No risk. I worked too hard, overcompensating. Low risk was not enough. I was going for *no* risk. When opportunities opened up, I accepted, for my own good, I told myself, even though it was agony.

I did well, but I wanted to break free. I wanted to *enjoy* being in the limelight. I always did like attention. So I tried something different: I pretended I was someone else—a self-confident, witty, good-joke-telling, indomitable woman speaker—Geraldine Ferraro. She was in the media a lot, and I had met her personally. She was warm and approachable. My break came when I gave a speech in front of a thousand people and live television cameras. I just pretended I was Geraldine. It worked. When I arrived home, my neighbor shouted out his front door, "Great speech! Your head and heart were in the same place." The magnitude of the situation seemed to prove to my nervous system that public speaking was not life-threatening after all. Now I am free to take some risks, be extemporaneous, off the cuff. Actually, I am a bit of a ham. Those are my best moments, my moments of magnificence. It had been a long, hard road home, back to wholeness.

My daughter is just like I was as a child. She is shy, an introvert, actually, in the sense that she feels most comfortable watching before she jumps in; she has a rich inner world and can entertain herself for an hour at a time. Socially, she likes it intimate, one-on-one, or with family. Angela knows Mommy goes to teach at night; she has seen me on TV and heard me on the radio. When it came time for her preschool debut, a concert for the parents, I expected she would look down at the floor with her mouth half moving or just stare out at us parents, with all our cameras flashing and videos reeling. But no, she was front row center. With her head held high, she belted it out. She led the group in anticipation of all the movements to the songs, even though she was the youngest in the class. When refreshments were served, several other parents were gracious enough to whisper in my ear: "Angela was the star." "What a performer!" "Angela was the best." Of course, this was all a bonus. Inside, I was having a private celebration. My whistle wound had healed.

"Getting What You Really Want" Wound

When I was five, my family drove the six hundred miles to spend the holiday with my grandmother and my uncle's family. It was a fifteen-hour trip by car. At that time, there was little thruway. It was an arduous journey, no doubt. I was excited about spending Christmas on the coast of Maine, but I had a major reservation: would Santa know where I was?

That year I wanted just one thing for Christmas. I was desperate for it—a life-sized doll. I watched very carefully as my parents unpacked the station wagon. "Couldn't be in there," I thought. Santa was my only hope. But how would he find me up here so far from home? Well, on Christmas morning, I was one ecstatic and wound-up kid. In my abandoned state, I danced with my life-sized doll, around and around. I ran, I shouted, I screamed for joy. My father shuddered. Eight wild children in a crowded, small house, down-to-the-bone fatigue, and worry about a limping car in need of repair made him look lost and out of place as he tried to read the newspaper in a ladies' rocker. As I ran past him, he gave me that "Enough!" look and said between his teeth, "Stop it." I was stunned. The joy was knocked right out of me. My joy and his stress collided. I felt shattered. This was Christmas. This was the time I sat on my daddy's lap and sang Christmas carols in front of the tree. I thought he loved Christmas too. It was so incongruous. I ran upstairs to the bedroom and sobbed my eyes red.

Fast forward to a forty-year-old woman. The phone rang. "Oh, hi." It was my good friend Martha. We small-talked for a minute, but I knew there was something on her mind, some tension. She sighed deeply and told me something I did not want to hear. It was the third major blow of the day, and it was only nine-thirty in the morning. I choked and could not speak. "Hello, Linda, are you there? What's the matter?" Martha asked. She waited. To my own astonishment, I blurted out, "When you get what you really want, bad things happen." "What? What bad things?" Martha asked. I described the rest of my morning. "Where did you get that idea from?" Martha asked. "I don't know," I replied.

A couple of things flashed in my mind, one of which was the life-sized doll incident. "Boy, you better reprogram that one," Martha said.

My friend and I are of the thinking that the subconscious is programmed by the conscious mind. The subconscious believes whatever we tell it as truth, even coming from a five-year-old girl. I wish reprogramming were as easy as pressing "delete" on the computer keyboard. I canceled my thirty-five-year-old decision this way: I replaced it with an affirmation, "Whenever you get what you really want, good things happen." I replayed the life-sized doll scene in my mind with a different outcome, and I visualized the desired outcome I wanted in my life right now. There, that should do it. Deleted.

Flying Wound

During college, I went alone across country to California to do a three-month stint of clinical training at San Diego Children's Hospital. Somewhere over the Rockies, I believe, I felt terrible. I felt like I was going to die. I lay down over two seats; the flight attendant gave me blankets and offered me a drink on the house.

After I safely landed and got to my apartment, I called my parents and tried to process my experience with them. "Well," my mother said, "you really haven't had much experience with air travel. When was the last time you flew in a plane?" The last time was the first, in a crisis, when my grandmother, my namesake, died suddenly of a heart attack when I was ten. Even with this awareness, air travel was never comfortable; I was one of those white-knuckled people. Grip and bear it. Then in my mid-twenties, I read about a woman who lost her paralyzing fear of flying by "white lighting" the plane, or encasing it in a protective shell with her mind. So I tried it. I white lighted everything: the plane, the navigation equipment, the control tower and its personnel, the weather, the pilot and copilot, all the attendants, and the passengers. I knew I had healed when I was gabbing away one time coming home on a small prop plane during a thunder and lightning storm with high winds. My children love to fly. To them it means escalators and moving walkways in the airport, pin-on wings from the pilot, a snack tray, and a new activity bag from Mom.

Birthing Wound

When I was giving birth for the second time, things went very differently from the first time. I had dilated three centimeters while still sleeping in my bed at home. By the time I got to the hospital, I had progressed three more centimeters. The resident on call was delighted. After she checked me, she said, "You are in hard labor now; you'll have this baby out within a couple of hours, if not sooner." This seemed impossible. Was she talking to me, the mother of the thirty-hour labor and C-section?

When I reached the time to push and the baby didn't just pop out after a round of good hard pushes, I was taken right back to the agony of the first time, the first birth. All of a sudden, I was in that labor, not this one. I thought, "Oh, no, not again, I cannot stand it, I cannot take it." This so distracted me that I could not focus my energy on the current labor. I began to unravel; my energy and concentration bottomed out. I felt as if I were flapping in the wind, like a sail loosened from its rigging.

The attending nurse felt my descent and responded to my "I can't do it, I can't do it," with "No one can do it for you." I wanted her out of my room. Who needs you? I turned my head away from her when she came close to my bedside. I looked out the open door. Where was my help going to come from? I heard none; I heard nothing. I continued to endure the labor but was not giving my all to the contractions; I had no anchor. I was not working with them. The nurse stepped back to give me space, a second wind perhaps. I struggled to climb out of my first birth and felt strangely caught between two times, two places, two births, and two bodies. Then I felt something happening, something different, someone coming. In walked the resident. She smiled at me confidently as if she were seeing me holding my newborn in my arms, feeding at the breast, rather than this unraveling, frightened, lost mother-woman-child stuck in the muck of her hard labor and trying to pull herself out with no lines. This shocked me into returning. I had something to focus on. I watched her; she trusted me; she recognized me, the woman who was going to deliver this baby in less than two hours. The resident squatted in front of me, cupped her hands together, and said gently, lovingly, and steadily, almost in a whisper, "Give me this baby. Yes, yes, ohhhhh," she breathed for me. "Yes, give me the baby." We were on a seesaw. She recited the mantra, and I pushed toward her hands, into her hands; I pushed back to this time, this place, this birth; she breathed, I breathed; we worked for about fifteen minutes together. "Now lie back," she said. "No!" I protested, remembering the back labor pain. Our rhythm broke. She laughed. "It's over." she said. "Now lie back, your baby is coming." It was a birthing and a healing.

Healing

An unhealed wound is tender. It still hurts. I took a bad fall off my bike last weekend. The wound is scabbed over. I am letting it heal in the open air rather than bandage it. Several times a day, my children climb up on my lap, and my husband bumps my knee in bed at night. Each brush with my unhealed knee hurts. So now what I do is avoid the pain by pushing my children away. I point to my knee as explanation. At night, I sleep turned away from my husband in self-defense and for a better night's sleep. I know the knee will heal completely in several weeks; the kids will be back on my lap, and I will be back with my husband.

These brushes with pain are the sting of the unhealed wound. We reflexively pull away unless there is no way out, like in the middle of childbirth. We never get through the pain to the place of healing because we do not know we are wounded; we do not know we need healing. It is never as plain as the scrape on my knee. I do not even know *how* the scrape on my knee heals. I just know it will, and it does. Incredible. All I did was wash off the dirt.

Dirt. If we wash off the dirt and leave the wound open to the air, maybe it will just heal itself. When I was growing up, we never wore Band-Aids. It is not that my parents did not believe in first aid or were overprotective and never let us run and take physical risks. We certainly did get our share of scrapes and scratches, on the knees, elbows, hands, and chin. But we were taught that once a wound was thoroughly cleaned, just leave it alone, keep it exposed to the open air, and it will heal faster. If you cover it up, dirt may get underneath and contaminate the wound. It will take longer to heal.

It is not the wound itself that makes us vulnerable; it is the contamination, what gets inside, that infects the wound and makes it harder to heal: things like dirty shame, germy guilt, or bacterial fear. Infections can spread outside the site of injury or incident and spread to our self-concept, beliefs, and life orientation.

Remember the sting of peeling off a Band-Aid, the way it pulled your body hair? The longer the Band-Aid stayed on, the more painful it was to remove it. The pain of removing the Band-Aid was as bad as or worse than the pain of the wound itself. When the Band-Aid gets peeled off, it smarts with whatever infected feeling we bandaged our wound.

Healing is a matter of letting it happen. Our bodies are programmed to heal. So are our minds. Life is organized to heal. To let healing happen, we must clean out the "dirt," whatever is in healing's way.

Whenever my children hurt themselves, break open their skin and bleed, we examine the wound and ask, "Is it superficial?" If a wound is "superficial," it is declared minor. We just wash it off, get a hug, and go on with life. If a wound is deep, if it cuts into tissue, muscle, or nerves, then we need professional help to heal. We need stitches, maybe even surgery to set the body right so it can again heal itself. The doctor cannot weave together the cells that make up body tissue and layers of skin. She cleans out and prevents any blockage to healing and positions the body in such a way that optimal healing occurs, in the shortest time, with the smallest scar. Therapists do the same thing; they help clean out emotional infections that are blocking our healing and position the mind in such a way as to open the door to healing.

I do not believe we can ever heal all our wounds, and there is probably no need to. Like everything in life, we have to make choices.

There are many ways to heal. Do and use what works; there is no one way. Healing doesn't have to be all serious and somber. It can be playful, like pretending to be Geraldine Ferraro or white lighting a plane.

I believe all healing involves self-responsibility, releasing, and forgiving. After becoming a parent, I can more than understand my father's stress on my fifth Christmas. It was a minor transgression; I'm sure I was back on his lap sometime that day. From the vantage point of being a parent, it is much easier to forgive our own parents. My kindergarten teacher was a good teacher; I remember she was sensitive to my shyness otherwise.

Unhealed wounds tend to surface in crisis. It is often during times of crisis that our wounds percolate up from the subconscious. Crisis is when we are faced with a challenge beyond our ability to cope. We lack the skills, experience, and resources to resolve it. Crisis resolution requires that we grow to a higher state of being and functioning. We may have to heal our unhealed wounds to get there. We may have to go through the fire; there is no way out but through.

To muster the courage to push through the labor pains of healing, we need inspiration, we need guidance, we need direction, some way to do the work, some method; we need a focus like the medical resident offered me, her hands, her voice, her breathing, and her centered presence and confidence.

There are lightweight wounds and there are heavyweight wounds. The lightweight wounds, like those I've shared from my life, may be healed with the support of family and friends, finding a tool to work with and a clear goal in mind. Heavyweight wounds, the ones that cut down to the marrow, need heavy doses of support from family and friends and professional intervention and management.

I do not believe we need to remember the time, circumstances, or people involved to heal our wounds. (I had to "remember" to tell the stories.) Sometimes that just distracts us, feeds the infection, and gives us an excuse for ourselves. It is probable that my stories were not the real cause of my wounds; they may have happened earlier or later in my life, and it was probably a number of experiences that I tied together to make my wounding decisions. These incidents are just the ones I remember. Another child might have never been affected. Nowadays some people joke when talking about a quirk in their personality or some unexplained feeling: "Oh, it must have been from my past life."

Remembering the incidents, the detail, is not the issue. Remembering alone will not heal us. Our memories are unreliable anyway. What we are left with are our perceptions, our programming, our decisions. It is the *decisions* we made about ourselves and life that are important. That is what stuck. That is what we must remember in order to heal.

We also need to remember our birth rights and responsibilities. As adults, we have the right and responsibility to know that we did not deserve our childhood wounds, we have the right and responsibility to heal our wounds so they do not infect our lives or our children's lives, we have the right and responsibility to find and fulfill our life purpose, and we have a right and responsibility to grow into the magnificent being we were created to be—our highest, most loving self.

19

SPARKLING EYES

The Queen of Jewels

I HAD NOT seen her in thirty years. She had forfeited a profit for my sake. Back when I was ten, I wanted a certain pin for my mother's fortieth birthday, but the price tag read $12.50, and the limit of my saved allowance was $10.00. Mrs. Hagan was an established jeweler on State Street, where people went for wedding rings and genuine birthstones. I was slightly afraid of her back then. She was tall and thin and had her skin on tight. Her hair was pulled back in a taut bun. The bands of her rings were oversized for her thin fingers. The gems hid on the palm side of her hand. Her man-sized watch slid up and down her forearm as she worked. Bifocals hung from a chain around her neck. Abruptly, without a word, she took my ten-dollar bill and the pin from the counter back to the register, putting on her bifocals en route. When she returned, she handed me a small brown paper bag she held tightly at each corner as if to say, "Now hold on tight, don't lose this." As I took the bag, I dared to look in her eyes. I managed to mutter "Thank you." Behind her bifocals, I think I saw something. She said nothing. She just closed her eyes and smiled slightly.

Today I was to select a new setting for a family ring, a diamond. It was for my fortieth birthday. No longer familiar with the business community of my hometown, I did not know any jewelers. "Why don't you go to Hagan's?" suggested my mother. I was shocked that she was still alive, let alone still working. How old *is* she? I wondered. In my mind, I was picturing a ninety-year-old.

Mrs. Hagan had moved to the edge of town. My mother dropped me off and took the children so I could make my choice in peace. As I walked out of the overbearing heat and humidity and into the cool shop, I heard the chimes ring the half hour. No one was visible, so I stood at the counter and waited. Within a minute she emerged. She was still tall and thin. This time she was wearing her jewelry and her skin on right. Her hair was held in a soft bun. She extended her hand to me; the watch was gone, and the rings fit. She tilted her head slightly to make eye contact as she asked, "How can I help you?" Each word she spoke was full and round. I handed her the ring. Mrs. Hagan took it between her fingers and turned it as if to catch the light, to make it sparkle. "Ah, it is lovely, beautiful." I had seen it as a small diamond engagement ring; she saw it in its full magnificence.

She led me into a small room that looked like someone's formal living room. She led me to an upholstered chair and invited me to sit. She showed me several settings that I instantly liked; they were contemporary and matched my wedding ring well. How did she do that so fast? I wondered. Yet I felt I had all the time in the world. It was hard to make a choice. I almost wanted her to decide, but she said nothing. She only highlighted one or two differences among the rings. I felt a little uncomfortable with the absolute peace in the shop only the clock ticked. Being with Mrs. Hagan was like having my long hair brushed, slow and even.

After our business was over, I waited near the door. My mother was late, no doubt detained with the children. Mrs. Hagan and I talked, and I revealed to her my connections to the area, my childhood, and the story of the pin, thirty years ago. She confessed she did that for people as much as she could, business-wise. Between phone calls, the postman, and customer pickups, she updated her life for me as if we were old friends: the passing of her first and second husbands and the move off State Street. Recently she had purchased a riding stable with her daughter. She told me its whereabouts and invited me to come visit with my children. I felt like I was in a time warp. Mrs. Hagan seemed younger, not older. During our conversation she said, "You know, I am so lucky that I will never have to retire like some do. I love my work; I love being a jeweler. I have always loved it." At age seventy-six, she spoke with the freshness of a novice. Life had not beaten her down. She seemed to be a woman at peace with her life and with herself and still fully engaged in both.

"How was Mrs. Hagan?" my mother asked, as I climbed into the back seat of the car next to my conked-out daughter and the spilled popcorn. "Sparkling," I said.

When the children were asleep that night, I told my mother how Mrs. Hagan seemed younger than I remembered her thirty years ago. My mother astonished me with her words. "That happens as some people age; the beauty that was always on the inside comes out to the surface. Her inner beauty came out. What is on the inside will come out as you age. You cannot control it. What you truly are will be there for all to see."

My mother had wanted to give me a special gift to mark my passage into midlife, a kind of rite of passage. She did that and more. She gave me a priceless view of aging. Rather than the image of wrinkling up, shriveling up, or rolling up, maturing is about turning inside out. First you grow up, and then you grow out, from the inside out.

For Young Eyes Only

I had always thought that sparkling was the exclusive domain of children, young children. When wearily unloading my grocery cart at the checkout one day, the clerk asked, without looking up from the electronic belt, "How are you today?" Instead of my usual "Fine," I said, "Okay, but not exactly sparkling." The clerk laughed. "I can't remember the last time I was sparkling," she said. The bagger, a woman who looked like she could hold down three jobs at once, piped in, "I don't think I was *ever* sparkling."

Then there is the more studied perspective. Several years ago I had an academic discussion with the principal of an elementary school. We spoke of those bright-eyed kids who enter school and then by third or fourth grade or latency, the spark seems to dampen like closing down the flue of the fireplace. I questioned why this happens to our children. "When children begin to become more abstract in their thinking and are developing a more cognitive approach to learning . . . moving out of the experiential and kinesthetic learning period, I think that is when we see a different look in the eye," explained my principal friend. I saw it as regrettable; he viewed it as inevitable. I saw it as a kind of shutting down; he saw it as moving on.

Losing Spark

I found that I did have company in my regret of this loss of spark, the sparkling quality. Once when I was in line at the post office mailing holiday packages, my toddler ran back and forth under a suspended rope that was placed there to keep us adults in line. He was delighted to have discovered this activity. He was having a sparkling time. A senior woman standing behind me smiled at my son saying, "Oh, she is so beautiful." "Thank you," I said. "*He* certainly is." We laughed. I turned back around, thinking that was the end of our exchange. "Whatever happens to us?" she asked. "We start out so beautiful and then . . . " I turned back around, looked at the woman, and scanned down the line behind us. We adults were all loaded down with packages, waiting in passive silence for our turn to come, a pause between the other errands and duties in our lives. I just gave the woman a "Who knows?" shrug. It was the kind of question I did not shrug off my mind, though; I tucked it away. It was a prompting.

So what does happen? Is the loss of our inner fire, our spark, a necessary part of growing up? For most of us, our eyes shine on occasion. They are like fireflies—you never know when they are going to light up. For some, the eyes just die.

Take Mr. Green, with the red curly hair. He was our new gym teacher in second grade. He was quick to wink. He smiled with his whole body. He was buoyant when leading our class single file down the halls and out to the playing fields for gym. His bulging muscles contoured his arms, shoulders, and neck which he put to good use for piggyback rides and carrying one kid on each hip sideways. In gym class, Mr. Green always corrected us privately, in a huddle. With a hand on the shoulder, he whispered new instructions. He only yelled to say, "That a way!" He seemed very big then, reaching out to us in all directions on the field. He sparkled.

I happened to see him again after I had my own children. He was supervising a summer recreational program on those same fields. My children romped around the playground. I would never have recognized him if we had not had an exchange over some older boys who needed some "new instructions" about playing around younger children.

He did not go over and huddle this time. Instead, he yelled across the playground. The boys ran off in a pack. His red curly hair had turned to a gray buzz. His muscles had hardened. He never uncrossed his arms from his chest. As an adult, I felt more hesitant with him than when I was seven. With reserve, I introduced myself. He remembered. But I had hoped for too much. My second-grade Mr. G. could not broad jump that far in time.

Reading Spark

We read sparkling eyes more than we may realize. It is the fastest way to check in with our children, lovers, and friends.

When parents collect their children after school, a birthday party, or a visit to a friend's house, they often will say, "I can see you had a good time." The child has not said a word, and the parents do not bother to ask; they can *see*. What the parent sees is the light in the eyes, the brightness in the child's being.

I had not seen my grandmother in over a year, since she had become seriously ill and was dying from cancer. When I went to visit her for what I knew would be the last time, she was unrecognizable to me in body. A large woman who had always been full in face and figure and beautifully groomed and dressed, was now emaciated, skin draped on bone. She honored me by walking, step by precious step, out of her bedroom into the living room. She sat next to me on the couch and patted my knee like she had done all my life. I looked into her eyes, the only part I recognized, and, my God, they were sparkling. Speaking was hard so her eyes spoke for her. "I love you. Good-bye, dear."

When you see sparkling eyes, you know all is well, at least in spirit. When you see flat, dull, or sunken eyes, something is off. It may be illness, despair, discouragement, or dispiritedness.

When we ask people, "How are you?" and they avert their

eyes and say "Good," we know they are not. Eyes never lie.

For a period of about three months when my son was six, he seemed to lose his sparkling eyes. They looked dull in comparison to what we were used to seeing. He was doing well in school and with his friends, but at home sometimes he seemed a little off, not his usual beaming self. We watched and waited, wondering if those magic years, that sparkling time of early childhood was over. I am happy to say that the sparkle did return, along with his effervescent personality. What changed? The season. That spring, our son's inherited allergies manifested for the first time. He did not feel all that great, even though there was not much to show for it except a stuffed-up nose in the mornings.

Window to the Soul

There is an old saying that the eyes are the window to the soul. I believe this is true, but what we often see in the eyes when we look in is not the soul but a shade.

In our youth, we focus on learning to survive in physical reality. Following the example of our caregivers, we develop our bodies and minds. Since spirit is not considered necessary for survival, it is not nurtured or even acknowledged as part of our makeup; it is seen as a kind of dispensable vestige. Regrettably, spirit becomes the sacrifice to our course in survival. But to be whole and magnificent, or wholly magnificent, we are meant to use all aspects of our being.

Picturing Spirit

Let's make a picture. If we were to stack a block tower of the levels of being, first goes body, then emotions, next mind, and spirit goes on top. These levels are meant to work as a complex system where every level is in constant communication with all others, the body-mind-spirit or the BMS network. If the messages on any level are to integrate with all other levels, we need to get hooked up, body to spirit and spirit to body.

The Star of David is an ancient symbol of the BMS hook-up. The upright triangle is the body reaching for the spirit, and the overlapping, inverted triangle is the spirit permeating the body. Earth to heaven and heaven to earth.

The Star of David also symbolizes the parent and child orientations. The child is the inverted triangle, the big spirit in a little body. The parent is the upright triangle, with a big body and mind but with a quiescent spirit. The overlap of the two triangles shows how a parent and child can cross-fertilize each other's lives. The parent creates a physical form or body for the child and teaches her to live in physical reality. The child, being fresh from spirit, awakens the parent to the reality of his own spirit as part of his whole being.

Children are more "being" than body or form. Adults identify more with body and form. But we are not just human bodies; we are human *beings.* We are spirits with a human form, rather than humans with a spirit. We know the difference on some level, for whenever we feel our limitations and shortcomings, we say "I am only human." But when we feel shortshrifted, our dignity has been stepped on, or we have been treated as less than whole, we cry, "But I am a human *being!*"

Developing Spirit

So how does the parent develop his or her spirit? We need a "practice" so we can learn from our mistakes and successes. Just like any kind of development, it involves trial and error, feedback, correction, repetition, practice, and then mastery. Some people meditate, practice yoga, recite mantras, write in journals, camp in the wilderness, or go on vision quests. These people are not parents of young children.

But parents still need a practice to develop our spirits. A

practice is something that you are totally committed to, something you do every day no matter what, whether you want to or not. You guessed it! Parenting can be our practice. It is the perfect practice. The search is over; it just climbed right into our laps.

My son's teacher knows his practice well. He will forfeit a lesson for the real practice of his profession. Posted on his desk is this quote from the great child psychologist Haim Ginott:

> I've come to a frightening conclusion that I am the decisive element in the classroom [insert "family"]. It's my personal approach that creates the climate. It's my daily mood that makes the weather. As a teacher [insert "parent"], I possess a tremendous power to make a child's life miserable or joyous. I can be a tool of torture or an instrument of inspiration. I can humiliate or humor, hurt or heal. In all situations, it is my response that decides whether a crisis will be escalated or de-escalated and a child humanized or de-humanized.

Keeping the Light On

How exactly do we practice? Leave it up to a child to tell us. Last summer a friend handed me a must-read entitled *And There Was Light*, an autobiography by Jacques Lusseyran. The author helped to organize the French Resistance during World War II and saved thousands of Jewish lives. He was betrayed and survived fifteen months in Buchenwald, the Nazi concentration camp.

Despite the extraordinary events of his adulthood, Lusseyran centers most of the book on his youth, which was no less extraordinary. At age eight, little Jacques became blind. This was a time of profound awakening for him. After some struggle, Jacques discovered that he did not have to live in darkness. But to have light, he had to be in a certain state of being. In a paradoxical way, his blindness taught him how to live "in the light"; it was his practice. The light and colors Jacques saw in his blindness were as real to him as those the sighted person sees. Lusseyran remembers when he first started seeing the light after becoming blind: "I was aware of a radiance emanating from a place I knew nothing about, a place which might as well have been outside me as within."[1] This light remained with him or he with it throughout his entire life.

Young Jacques loved the light. It faded or was extinguished only at certain times. He paid close attention and soon learned what turned the light on and off. Here is his list, clear and simple:

No light:

fear
anger
impatience
jealousy
greed
hatred
anxiety

Light:

love
harmony
kindness
friendship
empathy
service
interest
learning

Beyond having light and color, Jacques learned a different way of relating to physical reality altogether. In order to "see" things in his environment, he could not remain separate from them. As a blind child at age eight, he had learned the secret of oneness. "It is tuning into them [things] and allowing the current they hold to connect with one's own, like electricity. To put it differently, this means an end of living in front of [separate from] things and a beginning of living *with* them."[2]

Most of us are not blind; we do not experience such dramatic feedback if our "light" is on or off. But if we pay close attention, there must be something, some cue or sign. I get a tingle; it feels like the cells in my body are quivering.

When I look at Lusseyran's "light" list, it certainly covers the goals of parenting. The reason parenting is such a powerful practice is its intensity, its constancy, "whether we want it or not." In parenting, we get very clear and direct feedback as to whether we are in the light or not by our children's behavior. It is very, very hard work. Good parenting days are more light than not. I have concluded that perfection is out of the question.

Living with Spark

Back to sparkling eyes. People who live in the light, not that they are beyond darkness, but that they choose light, seem to live life on purpose; they possess an unusual drive to learn, serve, and create for the higher good. They work on harmony's side. I consider C. T. Vivian one of those people. He was a leader in the civil rights movement and a friend of Dr. Martin Luther King, Jr. Dr. Vivian was an out-of-town guest at our home ten years ago. He had a powerful presence and a contagious laugh. And yes, he had sparkling eyes. Recently, we saw him again at a Dr. Martin Luther King, Jr. commemoration in our state capitol building. After his speech, we went to greet him. Yes, his eyes were still sparkling. His hair had grayed, but his arms were open. He shook my son's hand and bent down to look into my daughter's eyes. After greeting our children, he said, "I can *see* you are all doing well."

I bet that those who have sparkling eyes see more than those who do not. They see the shimmer, the wholeness, the holiness, the magnificence of life. "For those who have eyes, let them see." They see like Mrs. Hagan, the jeweler who saw the great beauty of my small diamond and forever changed how I looked at it.

Children annoy us when they are toddlers and they stop at every rock, flower, weed, crack, and puddle, delaying the more important task at hand. We grow impatient because we are not caught up with what they see; it does not consume us, it is boring, and we have seen it a thousand times. But maybe our children are seeing something we cannot.

And they do. Barbara Bowers, Ph.D., author of the best-selling book *What Color Is Your Aura?*, was the first to substantiate for me that babies see and watch auras. Auras are "the most beautiful part of us," says Bowers, who never lost her gift for seeing the colors or auras around people. I was keenly aware that both of my babies, and I assumed all new beings, see auras. The newborn will cast his eyes over the head and around the shoulders, admiring the colorful aura of his parent. Many children draw colors, that we think are rainbows or halos, around their drawings of people. They draw people in different colors deliberately, not because it was the crayon they grabbed from the box. One day, at the age of three and a half, my daughter drew "rainbows" around the people in her drawings. I said, "Oh, so you see all the pretty colors around people." She said, "Sometimes yes, sometimes no." Sadly, I thought, "Well, I guess she is growing up, all right."

People like Mrs. Hagan, Jacques Lusseyran, and C. T. Vivian inspire us with their spark. We know by their example that spirit can be recovered if we lost it on our way to growing up. But it takes practice, and patience, and if we have children, parenting can be the fast track back.

20

MIRROR THE MAGNIFICENCE

LIFE IS A mirror. Our outer experience is just a reflection of our inner self. Whether one believes this or not, it is interesting to play with this idea for a while and see what happens.

This is certain: We are our children's first and most powerful mirrors. They are counting on us to mirror their magnificence.

Our children are our clearest mirrors. The image we see through their reflection is our truest self.

Seeing Our Mirrors

A mirror is a person or situation that reflects back to you your state of being. Anyone, even complete strangers, can act as mirrors for us, but we have to be awake. Here are some examples from everyday life.

Mirror 1:

I had been following the saga of Helen's struggle to get clearance from her health maintenance organization for her daughter's major surgery, which that she wanted done in another city by a prominent surgeon. "This is very hard, not knowing; the surgery is scheduled for next week, and we still do not have the approval letter. I have taken my daughter for a tour of the hospital and everything. I am on the phone all the time trying to get this straightened out. It is hard not putting my attention where I am most needed." (I presumed she meant on supporting her child and other family members.)

Helen is a pediatric nurse. "You know," she said, "yesterday when I was working, I got a very weird phone call. A father called and said his daughter was going to be admitted, and he wanted to know what to do. I had never heard of the referring physician and was not notified of any admissions. I asked if he had the right hospital. Then the panic started. 'I just don't know what to do,' yelled the father. 'My daughter doesn't want to come, but she hasn't had a BM in a week.' Helen responded, 'Of course she doesn't want to come to the hospital; no one does. But sometimes we have to do hard things so things will be better.'

"After I got off the phone, I thought, 'Wow, am I that crazy?' I think God sent me this phone call so I could hear my own counsel."

Mirror 2:

I was off schedule and feeling off key. When I turned on the ignition key to the car, nothing happened. Dead. After AAA jumped my car, I sped off to the city recreation department for the discount tickets to the water park. When I arrived, the secretary told me they only took cash. So, back into noon-hour traffic to the "Tyme Is Money" machine. While buying my ticket for a speed ride down a water slide, I was thinking of another kind of ride, a pontoon ride. "When do the pontoon boats go out?" I asked the secretary. She did not have the information. She called to a co-worker in the adjacent office. A fit, pressed-looking man with shiny loafers stepped out of his office. Without looking up from his papers in hand, he said, "The person you need to speak to is Chad; he is not here right now." "But I just want to know dates and times," I said. As he turned back into his office, he mumbled that he would try to find some information. I wondered if I should bother to wait. He was clearly annoyed at the interruption, and I was in a hurry. But I was committed now. So I waited and flipped through the glossy water park brochure . . . It was going to be wall-to-wall people, with temperatures in the 90s . . . the lines would be long . . . a hell of a weekend . . . but I had promised my son. I would just have to change my attitude, and I did, right then and there.

When the man finally emerged from his office with the pontoon schedule, I thanked him wholeheartedly. You would have thought that I had handed him a butterscotch malt. His facial expression lightened. The scowl was gone, and he managed a smile. "You are most certainly welcome," he said. He waited for me to leave before returning to his office. On the way out, I bumped into a hassled-looking woman who was probably picking up tickets on her lunch break. "Where is the ticket office?" she asked without breaking stride. I escorted her down the hall and pointed to a hidden stairwell: "Down the stairs and to your left." "Oh, thank you so much," she yelled back to me.

Mirror 3:

This summer three generations of us girls did some July Fourth shopping. To my surprise, I did find an outfit that was something more than just another top and pants to wear. I showed it to my mom in the dressing room. "How do you like it?" I asked. She said, "Hey, that looks really good. How do *you* like it? It is what *you* think that really matters; *you* are the one who is going to wear it." I went by the cashier's desk. "What do you think?" I asked the salesclerk. "Oh, that looks great!" (What did I expect her to say?) "Thanks," I said. "How do *you* like it?" she asked. (Not that again!) A young woman, in her early twenties, leaned against the cashier's desk and put in her two cents. "It doesn't matter what *you* think; it's what other people think that counts." Laughing, I said, "Hey, just a minute ago my mother said . . . " "Well, she is wrong," said the young commentator. By now, the conversation was a game and a kind of generational statement with me caught in the middle. And I was. Both are important because one plays off the other.

Magnificence Begets Magnificence

Magnificence that is mirrored creates more magnificence. That is what our children are looking for from us, to mirror back to them their own magnificence. They feed on it and grow on it. We have all experienced the surge of joy when our child comes running into our arms with the painting she made at nursery school or the ladybug she captured in her hand in the front yard.

A growing child does miraculous things with her intricate web of feedback loops and network of intersystems communication that make up the wiring of her nervous system. It is the feedback and intercommunication among the balance, position, visual, muscle, nerve, and touch systems that guide the child through the neurodevelopmental stage and bring her upright, victorious over gravity. It is feedback that refines the child's movements for kicking, pedaling, throwing, catching, drawing, writing, and speaking. The feedback that goes on between skin and bones is invisible to the eye.

But a child can only develop so far with feedback inside the body. She looks outside the body, to the environment, for feedback for her feelings of safety, security, self-awareness and self-esteem, and her sense of competence. She looks first to her parents to mirror the magnificence of her being beyond biology.

Children are born potentially whole. By this I mean that their magnificence must be nurtured into being. The life that we create for our children is the "body" within which they will grow and develop. We want it to be as magnificent as possible. We want the mirrors to reflect their exquisite beauty, trust, and love. But parents can only mirror for their children as much magnificence as they see in themselves. The more magnificence we see in our own mirrors, the more we can reflect back to our children.

Making Magnificence: Reverence

So how do you mirror magnificence? I believe you start with reverence. Each and every child is precious and worthy of the very best of ourselves. We must bring our best, our higher selves rather than our leftover selves, into our parenting as much as possible.

Parents with limited parenting skills or low parenting esteem feel out of control of their children, react reflexively, and blame the child for her "misbehavior." "You are a brat," "You are a bad girl," "Stop that or I'll spank you," "Come here right now or no TV for a week." We have all seen and heard it, limbic-level parenting, and we have even slipped into it ourselves when we were desperate or having a very bad day. So begins the unraveling, the tainting, the spoilage of magnificence. We are all too familiar with the wounded child and dysfunctional family movement, where adults are spending their prime years trying to heal childhood wounds that bind them to misery. It is a heavy dose. We are responsible for our children's magnificence or misery.

To maintain your mirror of magnificence, learn something about child development from the pros. We feel most reverent, most appreciative of things that we know something about. Being a reverent parent cannot happen by love and intuition alone. Having some skills and knowledge under our hats enhances reverence in our heart. Top on my list are pediatricians T. Berry Brazelton and Penelope Leach, child psychologists Haim Ginott and David Elkind, parenting experts Polly Berrien Berends, Adele Faber and Elaine Mazlish, and Randall Colton Rolfe, and learning expert Thomas Armstrong. So when our children climb out of their cribs, smear food in their hair, have a BM in a special place, write on the walls, dial long distance, or use our beds as launching pads, we will know that they are right on target, just what their developing bodies and minds ordered.

Let's face it: we want our children to reflect well on us as parents too. We must all admit to the pride we feel when people compliment us on our children. "Oh, he is so beautiful! She is so smart! How precious, so well behaved, so observant, how thoughtful!" We stand back and think, well, we must be doing something right.

These same children are also very capable at times of making us look bad. They throw a tantrum when it is time to leave the party; they scream whenever we get on the phone; they swear in front of grandparents; they knock down the supermarket display; they pick flowers for you from your neighbor's perennial garden; they do not discriminate between eating on a picnic and at a pricey restaurant; they insist on wearing their bathing suits to child care for dress-up day in January; they play hide-or-seek at the mall and you are sure they have been abducted.

When this happens, the reverent parent, the parent who has a healthy parenting esteem, protects the child in front of others: "Oh, she is tired, too wound up, too late getting to bed, too many transitions, over-stimulated, hungry, needs a nap, we left our manners at home." We remove our children from the situation as soon as possible. When on safe ground at home, we think through what happened. What is going on? What is the child telling me by her behavior? Is it just a case of a skipped nap, or does she need some information, guidance, boundary setting, rules, or correction? What could I have done differently? We view the incident from a management and developmental perspective rather than a case of bad behavior, bad child.

Milieu for Magnificence

Create as many situations for your child to shine, to be magnificent, as your time and energy allow. Give children the attention they need, so they do not have to be bad to get it.

Yesterday all four of us went shopping for some new linens. The big home sale was on at our favorite department store, and our pillowcases were frayed at the seams. Our children were predictably bored, as my husband and I tried to find our way around the bedding section. "Don't they have any white twin cases left?" I sighed. Our children were running up and down the aisles in a kind of tag game. My daughter was squealing with delight as her brother chased after her. The salespeople were watching as Toby and Angela cut close corners in the dishware area. My husband and I called to them alternately to stop running, slow down, and soften their voices. Nothing short of leaving the store was going to work. Nonetheless, I was not going home without new 100% combed cotton, 250 thread count, supercale, easy-care pillowcases. "Is it always like this?" my husband asked. "Why do you think I never go shopping?" I responded. It was my husband who finally took to higher ground. "Let's stop yelling at our kids and get out of here."

In the evening we all went swimming at the pool. We almost had the place to ourselves. We all jumped, splashed, and dove like playful dolphins. We sat on the bottom, talked under water, swam under each other's legs, had races in different strokes, did our headstands and rolls tricks. We laughed and squealed and shouted. The children were magnificent. Same kids, same day, same energy, same motivation, but a change of environment.

Children are magnificent if they can "do it," "be it." They are neurologically programmed for activity. They are all "hands on," interactive. They want to be the active ingredient of experience. That is how they learn best. When they must "behave," watch, be still, be quiet, wait, stop, or slow down, they have to quench their own inner drives that are set in place for their growth and development.

Less Than Magnificent

If our children are anything less than magnificent, it is because there is something wrong either in their inner or outer experience of life.

For instance, my son has allergies. If he has rolled in the grass, run into mold indoors or out, or enjoyed a windy day in fall or spring, he gets ornery, whiny, emotionally labile, short on patience, and high on irritability. The allergies steal his energy, too. He tries to push through but sometimes loses his steam. He can be hard to live with during those times. But I have to remember that life is uncomfortable for him during allergy season. He is just mirroring his inner experience despite lack of external reasons. My darling is in there, behind those allergies. He too wants them to go away so he can feel good again, but he is not in control of his autoimmune hypersensitivity. He just got the wrong set of genes. So we have our feedback to get more aggressive with the environmental controls, his medical treatment, and watching his diet and bedtime more closely.

Regression is a common reaction to change for all of us but especially for children. After our move, my daughter was invited to play at a friend's house where she had been many times. When we arrived at her friend's, she would not get out of the car. "What is this?" I wondered. I knew she wanted to play, but something was holding her back. "What would make it okay for you to stay?" I asked. "You stay with me," she told me. "Okay," I said, "for a couple of minutes." After ten minutes she would not release me, so we went home leaving a disappointed and angry friend at the door. I knew then that this child was reacting to our recent move, and though she wanted to play with friends, she felt most comfortable on home turf. Going to a friend's house, though fun, is still a stress, a social stretch. When home base is stable and routine, we like these stretches, these changes of scenery; they energize and stimulate us. But when we are under some stress, some major change, the stretch may be too much for today.

His Own Magnificence

Pretend for a moment that your child is adopted. You can stop looking for yourself in him. By always looking for ourselves, or Grandma Liz, or Uncle Dick, we may miss our child's special gift, his very own magnificence. I was surprised to learn that Mark, one of my son's friends, was adopted. His mother, Barbara, told me the story as we watched our kids let loose in the indoor playground on a snowy day. "Oh, yes, we got Mark after three years of infertility treatments. We just gave up and applied for adoption. We feel very blessed. Mark is a great kid in so many ways . . . " Our conversation wandered onto the respective interests of our children. "You know, Bob really wants Mark to play hockey and to get into sports. [Barbara and Bob are both sports-minded and very active.] Mark is marginally interested. He is sensitive and has a creative side that I want to support. He loves music and has quite an ear. This Christmas he could figure out carols by ear on his toy piano. I was amazed. I think he may have some musical talent. There is not an iota of musical talent in either Bob's family or mine. If Mark was our biological child, I do not think I would ever have believed that he was musical. At least I'm going to give him the chance to explore it, to go as far with it as he wants to. One thing about having an adopted child is that you just have to watch and wait to see what emerges. It is kind of exciting, actually."

Clear Mirrors

Children are our clearest mirrors because their vision is not clouded with beliefs, inhibitions, self-consciousness, and judgment. Who else is going to tell us that we have hair growing out of our nose or that our teeth are yellow?

As author and teacher Shakti Gawain put it, "Because young children are relatively unspoiled, they are our clearest mirrors. As intuitive beings, they are tuned in on a feeling level and respond honestly to the energy as they feel it."[1] "Children also serve as our mirrors by imitating us from a very young age. We are their models for behavior, so they pattern themselves after us. Thus, we can watch them to see what we are doing."[2]

Children tell us what they are feeling by how they behave. This dynamic is a powerful insight for participants in my parenting classes. If a family is under stress, children will mirror this in their own characteristic way by being wild, stubborn, withdrawn, easy to cry, whining, or demanding.

Once a mother called me, very distraught that her two-and-a-half-year-old toddler was "totally out of control; he has turned into a monster. Yesterday he went crazy when the wristband on his toy watch broke," she explained. "I tried to repair it with no success and even offered to go and get him a new one. Nothing satisfied him. This morning he was tearing around the house, and he knocked over a favorite lamp and broke it. This has never happened before." This mother was trying to find the right label to explain her child's behavior. She wanted a treatment that would fix him. After we talked for a while, she asked, "Do you think he is spirited or sensory defensive?" I asked about her family circumstances. The family had moved from another state just four weeks earlier. I told the distraught mother that I thought he was reacting to the move; it was a matter of displaced feelings. I gave her some suggestions to help her son feel he had more control over and order in his life. Two months later she called and said, "You were right, he is much better now. He has really settled down."

On the morning that my mother was to return home after a week's visit, Angela and I sat on the bed in the guest room and watched her pack. We were chatting about family relations and quizzing my daughter on the names of her uncles, aunts, and cousins and where they all lived. As I watched my mother's characteristic body movements, her familiar clothes-folding methods, the way she packed, dressed, and redressed, a feeling came over me. My daughter turned to me and asked, "Are you sad that Grandma Judy is going home?" She knew even before I did.

One time my husband and I were very frustrated with each other. It was over a fundamental difference in how we operated. Under usual circumstances, we gracefully allow for each other's differences and look the other way at minor irritations that belong in the category of "how you squeeze the toothpaste." This time it escalated; we were tired and had not taken proper care of ourselves. In the midst of our bantering, he said, "Oh, you can be stubborn just like your mother," and I said, "Well, you are acting just like your father." As much as we think we are all grown up and totally our own person, we can mirror our own parents, even in middle age. More than a couple of parents have told me, "At times, when I open my mouth to speak to my children, I hear the voices of my own parents."

The Power of a Positive Mirror

Years ago my son was working at the kitchen table on a Legos construction while I was preparing supper. I could feel his total absorption and his inner satisfaction with his building project. We had both worked in silence for ten minutes or so. While I was dicing peppers, he said, "Mom, I love you." I smiled and let the words hang in the air without any uptake. He mirrored his own feelings, his own self-love. I thought, "This is what I most want for my children. I want them to love themselves, so the world will mirror love back to them." A child will possess self-love if we mirror his magnificence.

21

BOUNDLESS LOVE

" HI, THIS IS Nancy [my daughter's teacher]. I'm calling . . . " I interrupted her. "Well, how did the birth go?" (I
couldn't wait: birth first, business later.) Nancy, a new
grandmother, welcomed the invitation to tell the story
again, the birth story. "Ohhhh," she sighed, "it went just fine,
everything was smooth sailing." There was more, much
more, in her voice. I waited to see if she would spill over.
Pause. The silence of risk. "You know," her voice cracked, "it
is such a mmm . . . " she stopped. "Miracle," I said.

Before I had one, I could never understand the baby ma-
nia. It all seemed overly sentimental and gushy. So what is
all the squealing about? My friend Katherine loves to visit
babies in the hospital when they are fresh from the womb.
She doesn't wait until the babe is home; it is too old already.

And I have friends who attend their laboring friends as coaches and will jump at the opportunity every time. Janet, a regal grandmother, just has to get her hands on those babies after Sunday worship. A baby never cries in her arms. She always thanks the parents for the "borrow." In our neighborhood play group, the mothers whose "babies" are almost too big for their laps go after the newest young members for their "baby fix."

What is so magnetic about these small, dependent, and demanding creatures? We are so taken with the infant; why are we so in awe of her? She is minute in size but magnificent in being. She is a big spirit in a little body. She is our close encounter with the spirit world, a fresh delivery from heaven. She gives off an aura, an energy, a power that fills the room, the whole house. We love to soak it up. With her sleeping in our arms, we feel peace, we feel whole if not holy.

For a child to be released into the world, heaven and earth must converge. Birth is a handoff from heaven. As Wordsworth said, "Heaven lies about us in our infancy." That is what my friend Katherine comes to honor at each birth. It is the peace and joy of Christmas, the mystery and hope of Easter, and the reverence and gratitude of All Saint's Day.

We feel a love that we have never felt before. It is divine love, boundless love. It is delivered with our babies. We are to raise our babes with it. Our friends and families shower us with baby supplies and equipment; heaven showers us with boundless love. All parents feel it on some level, but few talk about it. You can see it in their eyes and on their faces. Heaven has entrusted us with the care of another soul, the highest responsibility and most holy work undertaken in life.

We love our children with a power unlike any we have ever known, unlike we have ever loved another. It is the closest we can get to heaven on earth. Sometimes I amuse my children with Mommy's mantra at bedtime: "I love you with all my heart, all my soul, all my spirit, all my body forever and for all eternity." There, that should cover it. But still there is more. I tell my babes, "I love you more and more each day." Still more. It is nothing that I can contain within me, or they can hold within them, or we can keep between us or in the life that we share together. It is boundless.

Parents' initiation into this divine, boundless love is different from that of falling in love with a lover. Then, our lover is the source, the focus of our happiness, or so we believe. It is the other who is so wonderful, who makes us feel so good, so in love. But with our newborn, it is the miracle of life itself and the divine love that sends us soaring. Birth is a reawakening; it is remembering our own true self. It is remembering where we came from, our true home.

This remembering, this brush with heaven and envelopment in boundless love, is experienced as euphoria. It can last for weeks and even months.

It was during my time in euphoria after the birth of my firstborn that I tried to express this encounter with boundless love. I was breathless; I did not have the words to say how I felt. It was at this time that our pediatrician friend, the father of two grown children, came to visit us and give his blessing. I don't remember anything else about the visit except his words, "Our children teach us how to love unconditionally." What struck me was what he *didn't* say. He did not say they teach us how to love *them* unconditionally, only that they teach us how to love, unconditionally. Period.

I never liked the word "unconditional." It sounds so technical, a peculiar way to speak of love, an un-something. It is defining love by what it is not; no matter what, despite of, even if, regardless.

How did we come to this—trying to describe our highest form of love by what it is not? Because we live in a conditional, imperfect, and human world. Unconditional love is the exception. It is interesting that you never hear anyone talk about *conditional* love. I guess it is not very inspiring, or maybe it is because there is no such thing. Conditional love is not love at all; it is an oxymoron.

Most of the relationships in our lives are formed by certain conditions: where we live and work, our occupation, politics, religion, socioeconomic status, gender, choice of recreation and life-style, and the ages and activities of our children. In our conditional world, we align with those who can do something for us and we can do something for them. It's not a bad start, but it often stops there. One of my son's teachers once said, "You can tell a lot about people just by the way they treat children and cats." "How so?" I asked. "Because you cannot get anything out of them," she said.

In surveying all the possible human relationships, blood love seems to have the best shot at boundless love: parent-child, child-parent, sibling-sibling.

We are born into this world with a covenant: to be loved beyond conditions. We are loved not because of what we do or what we become. Just *being* makes us worthy of love; that is the covenant.

In parenting, it is inevitable that we will not always observe the covenant. We will know it when we don't, because of our own psychic pain. Unconditional love is an ideal, a perfect love. It will always be a goal and never a full reality. But we can shoot for the stars, and we might make it to Venus. And thank heavens for forgiveness. We can ask ourselves for it, our God for it, and yes, I believe we should ask our children for it when we mess up, so that we don't mess them up. "I am sorry when I got impatient with you last night at bedtime. I was tired and on edge. I should have put my grouch to bed with no supper. My grouch can be a real nuisance sometimes. She has nothing to do with you. Next time, I'll warn you when she is around."

To keep our channel tuned to boundless love is easy when a child is a babe. We do not expect anything from our babe; she is perfect just the way she is. All she needs is tender loving care, and she will unfold. We marvel at what she learns despite us; within just a few short years, she has learned to walk and talk. It is miraculous to witness. Becoming seems so easy.

As our children grow, it is harder and harder to put our trust in nature, to trust in our children and trust in ourselves. As parents, we get anxious; we start wanting things for our children. We want them to have every advantage, a head start. We want them to be able to make it in this conditional world. We know the terms all too well. There is tremendous pressure on parents to put our children in every program and class, from computer labs for tots to gymnastics. We want our children to reach, if not surpass, their potential. This is the post-modern way of survival. The fundamental job of parents in any species is to teach their offspring how to survive. Our children are programmed to follow our lead; they do it by instinct.

Our children pick up on the conditional world by the time they reach school age, if not before. They start to want things, too. They want things as if their survival depended on it. They want a sense of belonging; they want to fit in; they want the props of their time and culture.

Today's parents have a tremendous dilemma. On one hand, we want to prepare our children to live in this world, and, at the same time, we are in a tug of war with our children when they discover it. At least half, if not more, of parenting is countering our popular culture that markets broken innocence, violence as adventure, and the idolization of "superstars." Our children are trying to become part of the world, and we are trying to shield them from half of it. Mix the two together, and you've got conflict.

It seems paradoxical. We are closer to unconditional love with our children than in any other relationship, yet there always seems to be conflict. Unconditional love is not devoid of conflict—far from it. Boundless or unconditional love does not mean we let our children walk all over us; it does not mean we do not set clear expectations and limits. It means we provide daily guidance and stay very much in touch with their lives. It means that we are totally committed to working it out to the best of our ability, and if our storehouse of knowledge and skills does not cover it, we ask around and try to learn more. It means that we learn the very artful and skillful task of performing all of the above without messing with love. Children will test our stamina, patience, tolerance, skill, knowledge, wisdom, and our sanity, but love is off limits.

I believe that almost all human endeavors are motivated by what we think will get us "love": achievement, money, status, service, beauty. We compete fiercely for it but are not conscious of what we are doing. We muster all our strength to get it. We exhaust ourselves running after it. But, in conditional terms, "love" always eludes us. We are running after a shadow of love, an imposter, a mute imitation. We have confused conditional love with the real thing. Boundless love is inimitable.

Refuge

So how, in this conditional world, can we create a refuge of boundless love in our lives? In my experience, when people share a common love, then their relationship has a chance to move beyond conditions. It is easy for me to love nature, to love music, to love books, to love children, to love mystery, to love creating, to love flowers and gardens, to love hiking, to love water and swimming, to love learning. It is in sharing these loves that my relationships can take on a boundless flavor. Sharing a common love takes the focus off the relationships, which are so often laden with conditions. With Mary I share a love of nature, with Diana it is a love of creating, with Liz it is a love of writing and books, and with Emily it is a love of children and learning. In sharing my loves with others, I can see the love within them, and they can see the love within me. We come to see one another as loving beings.

Switching people onto love can be very practical at times; it can be a saving grace. Once when I was riding in the car to an out-of-town conference with a colleague, I was getting a headache. Cheryl was wound up. She was going on and on about the tensions among co-workers, anxieties about overwork, and changes in her office. I was starting to feel drained, and I wondered if I would have the energy for our long day ahead. Not fully conscious of what I was doing, I switched channels. I switched her off of fear and onto love. I asked her about her children. Well now, that was a different subject. She started talking about something she loved to do with her children: skiing. We were sailing down the highway now. I survived the trip, survived the day, and even had to start back early because she had to go pick up her kids. Saved by love again.

No two people can journey very far into boundless love without forgiveness. Without forgiveness, love would not have a chance. We mostly see the world through our own binoculars with their narrow field of vision and experience. It is inevitable that we will unwittingly hurt and offend at times.

Once at a social gathering, I listened to Jean tell Sue about her upcoming trip back home to Ohio, a seven-hundred-mile journey. She was taking the kids in the van. Jean was anxious about making the drive without her husband and facing the unresolved tension with her parents and particularly with her brother. Her face and neck reddened when she talked about her brother's wife and the way she had insulted the family, five years before. Since the blowup, her brother had been estranged from his siblings but protected by their parents. "I have not really seen my brother in five years. We had no contact when my children were born . . . my kids don't even know their uncle . . . it's as if he was dead or something." Jean wiped her eyes. Sue's voice cracked. "Oh, for heaven's sake, life is too short, don't mess around, don't hold out, drop the past. Let it go and make your peace."

Boundless love, quite simply, is the glue of the universe. I chuckle at the thought of the day when scientists have finally dissected the universe down to its most microscopic particle and put it back together again. The energy they will find that holds everything together, keeps the universe growing and expanding, and creates life in all its forms and dimensions is love.

Love by its very nature is ever-growing, all-embracing. Children sing about this in preschool in songs such as "Love Grows," by Carol A. Johnson: "Love grows, one by one, two by two and four by four, love grows round in a circle and comes back knocking at your front door." And there is the "Magic Penny" song by Malvina Reynolds: "Love is something if you give it away . . . give away, give away . . . you end up having more. Hold on tight and you won't have any, lend it, spend it, and you'll have so many . . . they'll roll all over the floor."

Adults make it more complicated. Years ago I belonged to a 6:00 a.m. church study group that reviewed current events from a spiritual perspective. We were balanced, males and females, all baby-boomer parents. There was one discussion that especially intrigued me. The topic was free will, a gift given to humanity. Free will is the key to understanding our purpose on earth and the greatest mystery of all, love. Our purpose is to live in the service of love, to embody love, to make it whole through deed. Love left to feeling is not whole love. We must come to this of our own choosing. Love must be our will. No higher power will force or demand it. Nor will it punish us if we do not choose it; we only punish ourselves and each other.

We are the greatest experiment in the universe, and the most at risk. Our mission is to demonstrate the great power of love, that it is the greatest power of All. Well, ladies and gentlemen, I am sorry, but we are not doing very well. We are a sort of embarrassment, actually. But all is not lost. There is hope, and despite the many places of darkness in our world, there are also increasing areas of light.[1]

It is our job as human beings not to just consume love but to create more and more of it. We are supposed to be a kind of love generator in the universe. Love does not come cheap; it takes energy and effort. Every parent knows this. One can be witness to great beauty in a tended garden or on top of Mount Cadillac or in taking delight in a laughing child. There is no sin in taking pleasure in great beauty and delight. Our magnificently beautiful world and everything in it was created to be enjoyed. The world was also created as a catalyst for love-making. If one loves the garden, the mountain, or the child by becoming one with it, then the love in that place or in that person will multiply and reverberate into the world and the universe.

Boundless love is not linear: I give it to you and you give it back to me. You cannot keep score with boundless love. Love falls on anyone and everything that is in its way or reach. Children know this; they embody love, they emit love, and they can click into it very easily. In any school, especially preschool, where children are allowed to be children, to express themselves freely, to be whole, you can sense a special energy. It smells inviting, light, playful, sort of like glue, paint, and Play-Doh® all mixed together. I work at my son's elementary school and Sunday schools. Children are uplifting. They love to create. I always feel energized and more alive after doing something creative with children. The combination of children and creating is a powerful catalyst for love. Children are meant to be in our lives throughout the life spectrum to keep us on track. It's too bad we are such an ageist society. Adulthood can be so humdrum.

Once my daughter asked me, "Mommy, do you love everyone?" It was one of those questions that you ask kids to repeat because you want to make sure they said what you thought they said. In my mind I shot back, "Certainly not!

Where did you ever get that idea?" (I really fooled her.) On reflection, I think she was trying to figure it out. She was asking, "How do we know who to love?" Do we have loved ones and not-loved ones? If we say we love certain people, does that mean we don't love everyone else?

We are meant to love everything: our work, our name, our car, our town, our tennis partner, our goldfish . . . to just love. It is not a matter of being *in* love; it is a matter of *being* love.

We think we need to reserve our love energy for the certain select few: our children, our mate, our parents, our siblings, our extended family, and select friends. We feel that, somehow, if we spend our love on others, we are cheating on our blood love, as if our love is finite and we have to be careful with this precious resource. Edwin A. Burtt, the revered Cornell professor of philosophy, wrote at the end of his life, " . . . growing love is not cramped, one who values expanding awareness will never forget his special responsibilities but he realizes that, as love widens its reach, exclusive attachments fade away."[2]

My mother tells the story of a neighbor who once helped her out when she was in great need. Janet, who had five young children of her own, took my mother's two babies and toddler for an entire day. She fed and bathed us while my mother quickly packed to make an emergency move with a sick husband who could not help. My mother still says today, "I do not know how I would have done it without Janet; she was a saint that day." My mother felt guilty that she would have no opportunity to repay her friend. Janet replied, "Just pass it on."

Boundless love is a hard sell. It sounds too amorphous, too free, too open, too much like one-way giving. But it does come back around, not always from the same people you loved, on whom you spent your love. That is one of the great misunderstandings about love and the reason why we are hurt unnecessarily. We expect love to bounce back like a ricochet. I love you, you love me. If we don't get it when and from whom we expect it, we are wounded and feel betrayed by love.

But boundless love always comes back knocking at your door. Boundless love is our one true home and identity. You do not have to look anymore. When you expect it to come from anywhere or anyone, when you put it in the foreground of your life, you can find it almost everywhere. The other day I was dealing with my daughter's pleas in front of the vending machine outside the skating rink where my son was practicing hockey. "I'm sorry, honey, I just don't have enough change," I told her. Jumping up and down to hold off the tears, my daughter protested, "But Mommy, you said I could have the chocolate milk!" A mother at the machine next to us took two quarters from her wallet. "Here, will this do?" she asked.

My husband is the sort of man who likes organization: everything has a place and should be in it. He willingly admits that he is oversensitive to chaos. It used to be that when he came home at night, he got in a foul mood when things were a mess, in disarray, and cluttered. This set off bad family dynamics. He saw the mess first and his family second. The mess colored the way he looked at us. I called him on it. Now when he comes home he goes right for us. We are his foreground, the clutter the background. He showers us with love and *then* moans at the mess. Our end-of-the-day family scene is finally in focus.

How our children teach us love is not always neat and clean. It is more often a mess. We have to look beyond the sticky hands, the Cheerios® all over the car, the spaghetti face, the trail of toys and clothes, the dirty hair, the snotty nose wiped on the shirt sleeve, the spit-up on your power clothes, and the jacket thrown on the floor. Children teach us to love unconditionally, even if we feel out of bounds at times. They teach us about boundless love, they do indeed.

22

BONUS PARENTS

WE ARE THE first but not the only parents of our children. Bonus parents come at different times through a variety of people. They nurture and mentor our children beyond our own capacities.

Parents are not only those who give birth to bodies. A parent is anyone who helps to create and nurture the mind, heart, and soul of a child or children.

A bonus parent is anyone who takes a special interest in you, nurtures you, supports you, inspires you, or guides you. Their only interest is in your best interest.

A bonus parent is someone who believes in you, gave you a chance, or opened a door.

A bonus parent sees your gift(s) and helps you see it in yourself.

A bonus parent does not have to be someone who is a generation older than you. A relationship with a bonus parent may be short term, or it may be a single encounter. A bonus parent may not be anyone you know or meet. A bonus parent may not even be a person.

Like birth parenting, bonus parenting is altruistic work. The rewards are intangible, at least in this world, the world that is turned upside down, the world where we walk with our heads on the ground and our feet in the air, the world where making things is more valued than making whole human beings. In fact, caring for children is barely valued at all.

There is another way, another world. In the book *We, the Arcturians,* Dr. Norma J. Milanovich dialogues with beings from another section of the universe that is more advanced than our own, in the sense that the beings transcended long ago their struggle with reality and the meaning of life. They work with light, energy, a concept of oneness, universal laws, and fourth and fifth dimensions. But what is relevant here is the way they care for their young. On Arcturus, the ones who care for the young are the highest and wisest in the land.[1] Care for the young is the most revered privilege and greatest honor in their society. It is irrelevant whether or not we believe the authenticity of the Arcturian story. What is relevant is how the story affects our hearts and our thinking. My reaction was this: "No wonder they are a more advanced civilization."

I believe that bonus parents are the universe stepping in from time to time to nudge us toward our life purpose and higher self. I do not know how the phenomenon works. Maybe bonus parents are an answer to our birth parents' prayers. Maybe it is during a growth spurt or struggle that the bonus parent appears as a guide or catalyst for change. Maybe it is the work of our spiritual guides. I see bonus parents on a par with angels. Not the ones with the white robes, outstretched wings, and halos, but everyday people, our relatives, our neighbors, our friends, and our teachers.

I noticed long ago that the people who knew how to treat children were the people whom I trusted with myself. People who are respectful to children, who treat them with dignity, talk up to them, and are genuinely interested in what they have to say, stand very tall in my estimation. Those are the people I not only want around my children but around myself as well.

They are the bonus parents of the world. They are the "keepers of the child," that part of us that resounds with joy, love, and light and casts it out into the world.

My family has always lived in a university town. My children's companions when Mommy is working have been college students, Ann, Diana, and Laurel Ann—young adults with their own inner children intact. They were not sentimental about children. Rather, they actively engaged in my children's world, fully and wholeheartedly. They are "keepers of the child."

"Keepers of the child" seem to stay in tune with the child at any age. They can harmonize in several octaves at once, the upper octave of the child and the lower octave of the adult. You know the "keepers of the child" by how they make you feel. You feel valued, light, special, taller, bigger, awake, happy.

"Keepers of the Child"

My neighbor was hosting a party on the Fourth of July. It was raining, hot, and very humid. With everyone crowded onto the porch, it was a very sticky affair. My daughter insisted that I hold her in my arms. She was needing air and did not want a surprise encounter with the family terrier, Henry, down below. Bill, our host, took note of this and offered to take Angela to another part of the house and show her some dolls that had belonged to his daughter, who was now in her twenties. Bill sat and talked with Angela in the room while she played. When it was time to leave, I found her sitting comfortably on the loveseat in the music room with Barbie® paraphernalia all around. Bill was still with her. He looked up and said, "Just in time, she was just starting to want you."

My senior friend Virginia, the mother of three grown children, is into books, children's books. She knows that books can become a child's friend. All children need friends, and all children need books, their own books. So she initiated a highly successful program for disadvantaged children from birth to seven years of age, called the Mother Goose Program, with the Vermont Center for the Book.[2]

On my son's first Christmas, Virginia gave Toby two cardboard picture books by Helen Oxenbury. That was the beginning of our children's library. Every year since then she has sent my children books, the most beautifully illustrated and award-winning books of the year. We have not seen her in six years, but she is faithful every Christmas. When the package arrives, I again tell the story of "Virginia from Vermont" to my children. It kind of opens up the Christmas season. We read these beautiful new shiny big books under the cozy covers at night and sing our carols.

We had just arrived at our rented cabin on Lake Superior. Bob, the owner, saw our car pull in and came across the road to greet us. He liked to talk about his place and the new cabins he had recently built. He acquainted us with places of interest in the Bayfield area. Before he left to let us settle in, he turned around and, winking at my five-year-old son, said, "Watch out for the bears; they come down from the mountain sometimes looking for berries." He closed the door and left. He must have heard my son's crying distress, for the next morning, he knocked at the door at seven and asked for Toby. Through the crack in the door, Bob slipped my son a heaping quart of huge fresh blackberries picked by his own hand just that morning. "Here, Toby, these are for you. I had to fight off the bears for them." Wink.

These stories are just brief encounters, with little or no contact, but they make a child feel special, cared for in the world by people other than his or her own parents. The world can be a safe place. People can be trusted.

There are endless stories such as these. But just remembering a few swells me with gratitude for all the bonus parents who have blessed my children's lives. The bonus parents who have gone the extra mile, who have extended themselves, inconvenienced themselves. Like our pediatrician, who talked with me on the phone for over an hour at 10:30 p.m.; our neighbor Anne, who spent the night sleeping on the floor next to my son's bed while I gave birth to his sister; and Margaret, who, despite her own overload with three young children, took my daughter on several afternoons so I could pack and write or write and pack.

When our children are young, bonus parents are people who give them attention, talk and listen to them, and care for them. It is when children begin to mature that bonus parents act as guides, mentors, counselors, and teachers.

Naming Our Bonus Parents

Review your own life. Who were your bonus parents? Teachers, coaches, Scout leaders, clergy, neighbors, uncles, aunts, camp counselors, grandparents, doctors, older siblings or cousins, co-workers, mentors. At last count I had twenty-seven.

It was Mrs. Cape who went with me into the operating room where my parents could not go. It was Mrs. Kelsey who stirred a love of making things with my hands, like ice cube candles and origami paper folding. It was Mr. Smith who saw my gift with children and hand-picked me for my first summer job. It was Mr. Berman, my flute teacher of six years, who opened the door to my first-choice university. It was professor Betty Boller who was a mirror for my mind. It was David Smith who showed me how to "see" the heart in the rock. It was Dick Aronson who saw the creator in me.

Sometimes a bonus parent needs to be more than a person. When I was growing up, my family lived within ten miles of Cornell University. Both my parents were alumni. Cornell has a beautiful campus; it sits up on a hill overlooking Cayuga Lake, one of the Finger Lakes, God's handprint in upper New York State. Cornell was our cultural center in an otherwise rural area. But beyond all that, Cornell was special; it was great. It was revered by my father in particular. Cornell was beyond Ivy League. It was in a league of its own. I had always thought my father felt this way because he had grown up in the area and attended both undergraduate and veterinary school there. Cornell gave him a way out of poverty. It was not until recent years that I learned that Cornell was a bonus parent to him. One semester in, he did not feel well and was suffering from a heavy case of malaise. He both worked and studied full time. He could not keep up. Finally, after he went to the infirmary, the real culprit was found. His bad teeth, from a boyhood baseball injury, had abscessed. The infection was treated, but he still needed major dental work to repair his damaged teeth. My father did not have any money beyond what he needed for school. So Cornell gave him the money for the dental work, not as a loan but as care worth thousands of dollars today. When he applied to veterinary school and the selection committee questioned his bad semester, a professor intervened and explained my father's undetected infection. He was admitted—an open door. He graduated first in his class.

Sometimes bonus parents come in surprise packages. For our first baby shower, my husband and I requested that our friends tell or write a personal story of nurturing. My friend Sarah wrote of a time she fell down the stairs in her home. A much-awaited family trip was canceled. "There I lay on packs of ice in the middle of winter. Suddenly, Bob [her husband] and Jessica [her daughter] breezed into the bedroom with our living room TV set and a rented VCR. They had several movies I hadn't seen and announced 'popcorn and movies time.' Now VCRs seem to be more a part of people's lives, but for me, it was a whole new concept and a brilliant idea!!! [This was in 1982.] Our bedroom is fairly small but we three were piled on the bed watching this wonderful variety of movies and laughing and crying and feeling cozy together." Husbands, wives, even children can parent.

Even our young friends can be bonus parents. Prior to my heart surgery at age ten, I received several new things in preparation for the big event—new bright-colored summer outfits disguised as pajamas, and a hair dryer (a big deal at the time). But Katie, my best friend, helped me jump the fence that I was facing in my life—a fence that was so high I could not see to the other side. One day when I was at her house and helping her do the chores, feed the rabbits and pony and gather the eggs, she said, "My rabbit is going to have babies about the time you are in the hospital. When you come home, I will bring you one." It was matter of fact. Life goes on, and so would I.

Then there are the children who have to parent to save their own blood. I met Andrea at a Writer's Institute this summer. Andrea is independent. She owns and operates her own literary agency. Knowing about my interest in parenting, Andrea told me about two states, California and Colorado, that require both parents (whether married or not) to take parenting classes and family counseling in all cases of child abuse or neglect. As we continued our conversation, Andrea told me she was in the process of adopting her four siblings, who ranged in age from six to sixteen. I was astonished. She was adopting them so her parents would lose visitation rights. The mother was abusive, and the father was an alcoholic and neglectful. "How old are you?" I asked. "Twenty-three," she said.

Our friend David was orphaned at the age of two years. His mother died, and his father could not cope with four children and his drinking problem, so he took off. The children were raised in an orphanage. Growing up was rough. But David made it to adulthood not only intact but magnificent. He is a very loving, compassionate, talented man who has a special gift and bond with children. He attributes his success in large part to his older brother, Bob, who tried to keep the siblings together as much as possible and shepherd them along in the right directions. Today, David always refers to his brother as "Mother, Father, Brother, Bob."

If it takes twenty-seven bonus parents to turn out one all-parts-intact, productive person, we need more workers! Our numbers are just too limited. Birth parents cannot do it all. It takes a whole village: coaches, Scout leaders, Sunday school teachers, tutors, club leaders, big brothers, and big sisters. With the majority of parents fully employed outside the home, there is even less parenting happening. The parenting thread runs very thin.

To parent, you do not have to give birth first. Here are the qualifications as I see them: be a "keeper of the child," appreciate one's own gift, possess a generous spirit in sharing one's gift, and have an attitude. Parenting is an attitude. Some bonus parents start early in life; they stumble onto it when looking for extra cash, like Ann, Diana, and Laurel Ann. Some bonus parents started with their own birth children and never stopped, like Bill and Sally. Parenting is not a role they play after 5:00 p.m. and on weekends. Parenting is a nurturing attitude toward others of all ages.

I used to be a bonus parent to more people than I am now. These days, my parenting is concentrated on my own two children. But I look forward to the day when my time and energy open up a bit. It is already happening—a care call here and there, a thoughtful note now and then.

Bonus parents never know the good they have done, the service, the inspiration, the guidance, the care. Mine will never know unless they read this book. Thank you, all twenty-seven!

23

A PARENT'S REACH

PARENTS ARE POWERFUL people. The parent-child relationship is probably the most influential in our lives. Parents give us our starting place and a point of view on the world and ourselves.

No matter where on the continuum of love and respect we would place our parents, we carry them with us wherever we go. Whether we are a chip off the old block or are madly running away from our roots, our parents are always with us. It does not matter whether we have lots of contact, little, or none, whether we talk on the phone every day or see them once a year. It does not matter whether they are dead or alive. It does not matter because our parents are part of us; we absorbed them like a sponge in water.

Until we catch on and become conscious of the stowaway parent lurking in our psyche, our parent(s) always sits on our shoulder. Even as adult children, we are either seeking approval from our parents, rebelling against them, competing with them, or shunning, showing, surpassing, emulating, or fulfilling their dreams. Our stowaway parent is not the identical twin of our real parent, though a sibling maybe. Our stowaway is probably a blend of our mother and father, our ideal parent, and our own projections.

We always need "parenting." The idea is to transform our stowaway parent into a servant of our highest aspirations. Depending on our own level of maturation, our stowaway parent can have different faces and play different roles: The Judge, Our Conscience, Our Guide, The Higher Self.

According to psychologist James Redfield, author of *The Celestine Prophecy*, parents present their children with a dilemma to reconcile. The child must synthesize the different life perspectives of each parent into a higher truth than either parent stood for alone.[1] When we do this work, we move ahead; we become more whole.

Up until we experience our spiritual midlife, the different life orientations of our mother and father sit like oil on water; they do not mix. At times we are guided by the orientation of one parent and at other times by the other. But we always feel a split. To choose one parent's orientation over the other is a cop-out. It never feels quite right; we haven't done our work. We feel unfinished. Then in our spiritual midlife, usually somewhere between our mid-thirties and mid-fifties, when we are struggling to become whole, part of our work is to resolve or even dissolve our mother's and father's orientations so the two can be fused into a new whole. Then we become whole too. We have done our work.

Traditionally, it is the father/male role that represents the body and mind, and the mother/female represents the heart and spirit. We all know the pain that this split caused for both father and mother, woman and man. Our generation has been handed the task to sew back the seam of this split made centuries ago, and our children will do more.

There are those who believe that we actually choose our parents prior to reincarnation because of what we need to learn from them. Whether one believes the reality of this concept or not, it can be insightful and empowering to consider: "Why would I choose my parents? What have I learned from them? What were their greatest values? How do they apply to my life now?"

One strong catalyst for this work is the death of a parent. When a parent leaves us, at least in body, we must articulate what he taught us, what she stood for, where he found meaning in his life, what she committed to, the struggles he overcame. Our rituals of passage help us do the work: writing the obituary, selecting the setting, and creating the memorial service, selecting the music, prose, poetry, or favorite Scripture readings. Today it is not uncommon for adult children to eulogize their parent's life. Then come donations, scholarships, and other special tributes to their lives. I remember how my brothers, mother, and I struggled to describe in a few short lines the budding qualities of a scholarship recipient who would exemplify my father's character. To keep our parent close, we search for expressions of his values and loves; we make room for him to live on through us.

My father loved government. He knew how to work the system to make things happen, to get things done in service to his community. Over a thirty-year period, he served his community in elected and appointed positions. Two months after his death, I ran for the municipal school board in my city and served two terms. My father expressed his spirituality through his reverence for and love of living things. Biology was his proof of divinity. Six months after his death, I was pregnant with my first child.

When a parent passes on, our spiritual beliefs are tested. Like birth, death is a rendezvous with spirit. Just as in birth, there is the pain of separation, the exhaustion of laboring our grief; there is also the euphoria as we are showered with divine love once again. In birth, we are delivered to earth; in death we are delivered to heaven. For a moment, the barriers are broken, out flow the waters of the womb, and out flow the tears of our grief. Birth and death are made of the same stuff. My father's death came within two days of his birthday. At first this seemed incongruous, hard. That was before I knew about birth. Now I understand; I got the message.

Before my father's passing, I believed in eternal life. Now I know. A parent's love is eternal. In fact, parenting seems to be too. When a parent is set free, free from the demands of earthly survival and responsibilities, he or she calls us to freedom too. Because we are so bonded, parent and child, when our parent is set free, it sets something free in us too. "Do not hold back in fear; there is nothing to lose; you won't even lose your life!" It is like people who recover from a near death experience; because they no longer fear death, they no longer fear life either. On the other side, a parent can see you more clearly; he knows your life purpose. He does not want you to be him; he wants you to be you in all your full magnificence. He wants you to make your heaven on earth right now! He wants your spirit to soar. He may even seem a little impatient about it!

For some, our parents in heaven come to us in dreams. Others feel an undeniable presence, usually when we are alone and undistracted. Several months after her mother died, my friend Liz told me about her mother's call. One summer evening, Liz was resting on her back near a woodland, looking out at a stretch of red sky. A whippoorwill's vigorous cry caught her attention. The bird fluttered into the grove of trees next to her. "There was no doubt in my mind," Liz said. "It was her." (I understood her to mean that the bird was a messenger for her mother, in a form Liz could and would receive.)

Another friend said that when she takes a walk in the

woods, something her grandfather used to do every day, at times she feels buoyed, almost as if she is walking on air. She knows it is her grandfather. "I always feel much better; I feel at peace, like everything is going to be okay."

These connections with our parents on the other side are made most easily through love. Remember, love is boundless; it cuts across all barriers of time and space. We can connect best around a shared love, such as a special place, nature, music, wildlife, pets, or even sports. Wherever the territory is familiar, we are more sure when we have connected.

To *believe* in our connections, we have to reach beyond the physical limitations and "realities" that we learned while growing up. These boundaries are created by humankind's split of body, mind, and spirit. This split is an illusion, a lie. Just as we need to synthesize our parents' different life orientations to become whole, so do we need to reunite and synthesize our minds, bodies, and spirits to reclaim our wholeness and be set free once again. I believe this is the collective purpose of our generation, that our children will build upon. It is time to know once again who we are in our full magnificence.

Collectively, as a society, we are starving for spirit; we whine from hunger pains; we are malnourished. While we are struggling to find food for the spirit to fuel our daily lives, relationships, work, and world, we may find it right under our noses or sitting on our laps. It is something we have overlooked for so long we hardly recognize it. It will be through the wholehearted, wholebodied, and whole-minded care of our own and collective children that we will find our way back to spirit. Our children are here to teach us. They can help us grow whole. Stand aside and make room. Here they come: *BIG SPIRITS in Little Bodies.*

Endnotes

Part I: Bumpy Bliss
Chapter 3
1. "Staying Home with the Kids Pays Off," Cheryl Jarvis, *Wall Street Journal,* 8.31.93, p. 2.
2. "Tough Choices, Great Rewards," Sylvia Ann Hewlett, *Parade,* 7.17.94, p. 4.
   National Parenting Association
   P.O. Box 20280
   Dept. P
   Bloomington, MN 55420
3. "Jacqueline Kennedy Onassis Is Buried," R. W. Apple, Jr., *New York Times,* 5.24.94, p. 1.

Chapter 4
1. *Kything: The Art of Spiritual Presence,* Louis M. Savary and Patricia H. Berne, p. 17.
2. "The Possible Parent," Speaker: Sandy Queen, sponsored by Meriter Women's Health Center, Meriter Hospital, Madison, Wisconsin, 10.19.93.
3. "The Spirited Child as a Patient," Speaker: Mary Sheedy Kurcinka, sponsored by the Pediatric Department, University of Wisconsin Children's Hospital, 5.27.93.
4. Interview with David Elkind, Ph.D., by Linda Crispell Aronson, Wisconsin Academy of Pediatrics Annual Meeting, Egg Harbor, 5.10.91.

Chapter 5
1. Lines from the song "The Music of the Night" from *The Phantom of the Opera,* Lyrics: Charles Hart, Music: Andrew Lloyd Webber, Book: Polygram, Inc., 1990.

Chapter 6
1. *Technologies for Creating,* Robert Fritz, p. 79.
2. *Ibid.*

3. *The Path of Least Resistance,* Robert Fritz, p. 147.

Chapter 7
1. "Nurturing Growth Through Family," Gary C. Rummler, *Milwaukee Journal,* 4.29.94, p. 1D.
2. *Flow,* Mihaly Csikszentmihalyi.
3. "Learning Too Early May Kill Your Child's Fire," Linda Aronson, *Capital Times,* 5.28.91, p. 3D.
4. *You Can Postpone Anything But Love,* Randall Colton Rolfe, p. xxix.
5. *A Mother's Work,* Deborah Fallows, p. 31.

Part II: Growth Spurts
Chapter 9
1. "Where Mind and Body Meet," Speaker: Myrin Borysenko, Ph.D., Conference in Psychoneuroimmunology, University of Wisconsin, Madison, 10.26-27.93.
2. *The Shrinking of Treehorn,* Florence Parry Heide.
3. *Staying Home: From Full-Time Professional to Full-Time Parent,* Darcie Sanders and Martha M. Bullen, p. 33.

Chapter 10
1. "The Possible Parent," Speaker: Sandy Queen, sponsored by Meriter Women's Health Center, Meriter Hospital, Madison, Wisconsin, 1.15.92.
2. "Are You Pushing Your Kids?", Linda Aronson, *Metro-Parent* (Milwaukee), 9.91, p. 34.
3. "The Case Against Competition," talk with Alfie Kohn, Noetic Sciences Collection, Sausalito, Institute of Noetic Sciences, 1991, pp. 84-92.
4. *Ibid.,* p. 30.
5. "Are You Pushing Your Kids?" p. 17.
6. "The Case Against Competition," p. 86.
7. *Ibid.,* p. 90.

Chapter 11
1. *Gifts Differing,* Isabel Briggs Myers and Peter B. Myers, p. 7.

Chapter 12

1. *Getting the Love You Want,* Harville Hendrix,

Chapter 13

1. *Liberated Parents, Liberated Children,* Adele Faber and Elaine Mazlish, pp. 67-88.

Chapter 14

1. Personal Ponies Limited, Inc.
   Black Walnut Stud
   Greystone Farm
   430 Caswell Road
   Freeville, NY 13068
2. *Secrets of a Very Good Marriage: Lessons from the Sea,* Sherry Suib Cohen, p. 106.
3. *Ibid.,* p. 132.

Chapter 15

1. *New Traditions,* Susan Abel Lieberman, pp. 187-88.
2. *Ibid.,* p. 189.

Part II: Growing Whole
Chapter 16

1. "The Heart of Healing: Exploring the Spirit of Wholeness," interview with Rachel Naomi Remen, M.D., and Dean Ornish, M.D., San Francisco, New Dimensions Radio, tape 2373.

Chapter 17

1. "Advice on Child Care from, of All People, a Mother and Doctor," by Carol Lawson, *New York Times,* 6.13.91, B1.
2. *Coming into Our Own,* Mark Gerzon, p. 103.
3. *Two-Part Invention,* Madeleine L'Engle, p. 181.

Chapter 19

1. *And There Was Light,* Jacques Lusseyran, p. 16.

Chapter 20
1. *Living in the Light,* Shakti Gawain, p. 120.
2. *Ibid.,* p. 121.

Chapter 21
1. *We, the Arcturians,* Dr. Norma J. Milanovich.
2. *Light, Love and Life,* Edwin A. Burtt, p. 52.

Chapter 22
1. *We, the Arcturians,* Dr. Norma J. Milanovich, p. 55.
2. Mother Goose Program
   Vermont Center for the Book
   P.O. Box 441
   Chester, VT 05144

Chapter 23
1. *The Celestine Prophecy,* James Redfield, p. 147.

Bibliography

Armstrong, Thomas, Ph.D. *Awakening Your Child's Natural Genius: Enhancing Curiosity, Creativity, and Learning Ability.* Los Angeles: Jeremy P. Tarcher, Inc., 1991.

Armstrong, Thomas, Ph.D. *In Their Own Way: Discovering and Encouraging Your Child's Personal Learning Style.* Los Angeles: Jeremy P. Tarcher, Inc., 1987.

Baldwin, Rahima. *You Are Your Child's First Teacher.* Berkeley, Calif.: Celestial Arts, 1989.

Berends, Polly Berrien. *Whole Child/Whole Parent.* New York: Harper and Row, Publishers, 1983.

Borysenko, Joan, Ph.D. *Minding the Body, Mending the Mind.* New York: Bantam Books, 1987.

Bowers, Barbara. *What Color Is Your Aura?* New York: Pocketbooks, 1989.

Brazelton, T. Berry. *Touchpoints: Your Child's Emotional and Behavioral Development.* Reading, Mass.: Addison-Wesley Publishing Company, 1992.

Burtt, Edwin A. *Light, Love and Life.* Ithaca, N.Y.: The Gregory Paul Press.

Cohen, Sherry Suib. *Secrets of a Very Good Marriage: Lessons from the Sea.* New York: Carol Southern Books, 1993.

Corda, Murshida Vera Justin. *Cradle of Heaven.* Lebanon Springs, New York: Omega Press, 1987.

Csikszentmihalyi, Mihaly. *Flow: The Psychology of Optimal Experience.* New York: HarperCollins Publishers, 1990.

Elkind, David. *Miseducation: Preschoolers at Risk.* New York: Alfred A. Knopf, 1987.

Elkind, David. *The Hurried Child: Growing Up Too Fast Too Soon.* Reading, Mass.: Addison-Wesley Publishing Company, 1981.

Elkind, David. *Ties That Stress: The New Family Imbalance.* Cambridge: Harvard University Press, 1994.

Estes, Clarissa Pinkola, Ph.D. *Women Who Run with the Wolves.* New York: Ballantine Books, 1992.

Faber, Adele, and Mazlish, Elaine. *How to Talk So Kids Will Listen and Listen So Kids Will Talk.* New York: Avon Books, 1980.

Faber, Adele, and Mazlish, Elaine. *Liberated Parents, Liberated Children: Your Guide to a Happier Family.* New York: Avon Books, 1974.

Faber, Adele, and Mazlish, Elaine. *Siblings Without Rivalry: How to Help Your Children Live Together So You Can Live Too.* New York: Avon Books, 1987.

Fallows, Deborah. *A Mother's Work.* Boston: Houghton Mifflin Company, 1985.

Fritz, Robert. *Creating.* New York: Fawcett Columbine, 1991.

Fritz, Robert. *The Path of Least Resistance: Principles for Creating What You Want to Create.* Salem, Mass.: Stillpoint Publishing, 1984.

Gawain, Shakti. *Living in the Light: A Guide to Personal and Planetary Transformation.* San Rafael, Calif.: Whatever Publishing, Inc., 1986.

Gerzon, Mark. *Coming into Our Own: Understanding the Adult Metamorphosis.* New York: Delacorte Press, 1992.

Ginott, Dr. Haim G. *Between Parent and Child: New Solutions to Old Problems.* New York: Avon Books, 1956.

Heide, Florence Parry. *The Shrinking of Treehorn.* New York: Holiday House, 1971.

Hendrix, Harville. *Getting the Love You Want: A Guide for Couples.* New York: Harper Perennial, 1990.

Hewlett, Sylvia Ann. *When the Bough Breaks: The Cost of Neglecting Our Children.* New York: Harper Perennial, 1993.

Kohn, Alfie. *No Contest: The Case Against Competition.* Boston: Houghton Mifflin Company, 1986.

Kolbenschlag, Madonna. *Lost in the Land of Oz: The Search for Identity and Community in American Life.* San Francisco: Harper and Row, Publishers, 1988.

Kurcinka, Mary Sheedy. *Raising Your Spirited Child: A Guide for Parents Whose Child Is More Intense, Sensitive, Per-*

ceptive, Persistent, Energetic. New York: HarperCollins Publishers, 1991.

Lawrence, Gordon. *People Types and Tiger Stripes: A Practical Guide to Learning Styles.* Gainesville, Fla.: Center for Applications of Psychological Type, Inc., 1979.

Leach, Penelope. *Children First: What Our Society Must Do—and Is Not Doing—for Our Children Today.* New York: Alfred A. Knopf, 1994.

Leach, Penelope. *Your Baby and Child: From Birth to Age Five.* New York: Alfred A. Knopf, 1979.

L'Engle, Madeleine. *A Circle of Quiet.* San Francisco: HarperSanFrancisco, 1972.

L'Engle, Madeleine. *Two-Part Invention: The Story of a Marriage.* New York: HarperCollins Publishers, 1988.

Lieberman, Susan Abel. *New Traditions: Redefining Celebrations for Today's Family.* New York: Farrar, Straus and Giroux, 1991.

Lusseyran, Jacques. *And There Was Light.* New York: Parabola Books, 1987.

Milanovich, Dr. Norma J. *We, the Arcturians (A True Experience).* Albuquerque: Athena Publishing, 1990.

Murphy, Elizabeth. *The Developing Child: Using Jungian Type to Understand Children.* Palo Alto: Consulting Psychologists Press, Inc., 1992.

Myers, Isabel Briggs, and Myers, Peter B. *Gifts Differing: Understanding Personality Type.* Palo Alto: Consulting Psychologists Press, Inc., 1980.

Pearce, Joseph Chilton. *Evolution's End: Claiming the Potential of Our Intelligence.* San Francisco: HarperSanFrancisco, 1992.

Redfield, James. *The Celestine Prophecy: An Adventure.* Hoover, Ala.: Satori Publishing, 1993.

Rolfe, Randall Colton. *You Can Postpone Anything but Love.* New York: Warner Books, 1985.

Sanders, Darcie, and Bullen, Martha M. *Staying Home: From Full-Time Professional to Full-Time Parent.* Boston:

Little, Brown and Company, 1993.

Savary, Louis M., and Berne, Patricia H. *Kything: The Art of Spiritual Presence.* New York: Paulist Press, 1988.

Schlemmer, Phyllis V., and Jenkins, Palden. *The Only Planet of Choice: Essential Briefings from Deep Space.* Bath, U.K.: Gateway Books, 1993.

About the Author

After growing up in body and mind, Linda Crispell Aronson traversed the spectrum of human development from infancy through adulthood as a pediatric occupational therapist and adult educator. She holds degrees from Tufts University and The University of Vermont in Organizational and Human Development. As an adult, Linda has sought to reclaim her "big spirit," give it air and light, and exercise it in everyday life for a high purpose.

When Linda became a parent a decade ago, her search was over. Today she says, "The most powerful catalyst for igniting my spirit climbed right into my lap. Parenting has taken me deeper into life than I ever dreamed possible. My children have brought me life I never touched before, never knew existed."

Linda uses her "big spirit" in parenting, writing, and teaching. "When there is an opening, I power walk with friends, read on the fly, date my husband, have a fifteen-hour sleepathon once a month, and bike pulling a buggy."

Linda lives with her husband, Richard, and their two children in Madison, Wisconsin.

What Is A.R.E.?

The Association for Research and Enlightenment, Inc. (A.R.E.®), is the international headquarters for the work of Edgar Cayce (1877-1945), who is considered the best-documented psychic of the twentieth century. Founded in 1931, the A.R.E. consists of a community of people from all walks of life and spiritual traditions, who have found meaningful and life-transformative insights from the readings of Edgar Cayce.

Although A.R.E. headquarters is located in Virginia Beach, Virginia—where visitors are always welcome—the A.R.E. community is a global network of individuals who offer conferences, educational activities, and fellowship around the world. People of every age are invited to participate in programs that focus on such topics as holistic health, dreams, reincarnation, ESP, the power of the mind, meditation, and personal spirituality.

In addition to study groups and various activities, the A.R.E. offers membership benefits and services, a bimonthly magazine, a newsletter, extracts from the Cayce readings, conferences, international tours, a massage school curriculum, an impressive volunteer network, a retreat-type camp for children and adults, and A.R.E. contacts around the world. A.R.E. also maintains an affiliation with Atlantic University, which offers a master's degree program in Transpersonal Studies.

For additional information about A.R.E. activities hosted near you, please contact:

A.R.E.
67th St. and Atlantic Ave.
P.O. Box 595
Virginia Beach, VA 23451-0595
(804) 428-3588

A.R.E. Press

A.R.E. Press is a publisher and distributor of books, audiotapes, and videos that offer guidance for a more fulfilling life. Our products are based on, or are compatible with, the concepts in the psychic readings of Edgar Cayce.

We especially seek to create products which carry forward the inspirational story of individuals who have made practical application of the Cayce legacy.

For a free catalog, please write to A.R.E. Press at the address below or call toll free 1-800-723-1112. For any other information, please call 804-428-3588.

A.R.E. Press
Sixty-Eighth & Atlantic Avenue
P.O. Box 656
Virginia Beach, VA 23451-0656

Discover for Yourself

the Wealth of Insights Contained in the Edgar Cayce Material...

Throughout his life, Edgar Cayce (1877-1945) was able to display powers of perception that extended beyond the five senses. He was guided by one solitary goal: to be helpful to people, and he used his talents of psychic perception to provide practical guidance for thousands of individuals.

The Edgar Cayce legacy contains information on more than 10,000 different subjects in the areas of healing, holistic health, spirituality, meditation, philosophy, reincarnation, dream interpretation, and prophecy. He has been called a philosopher, the most gifted psychic of all times, and the father of the holistic health movement. More than 300 books have been written about his work!

In 1931, Cayce founded the Association for Research and Enlightenment, Inc. (A.R.E.) to study and research this information. Today, the A.R.E. is an open-membership organization–made up of thousands of individuals around the world–that offers conferences, seminars, research projects, newsletters, and small group activities. For information, call 1-800-333-4499, or use the card below.

☐ Enroll me as a member of A.R.E. (Edgar Cayce's Association for Research and Enlightenment, Inc.) I enclose $40.00 (Outside U.S.A. add $15.00 postage.)

**VISA or Master Card CALL TOLL FREE
1-800-333-4499, 24 hours a day, 7 days a week**

You may cancel at any time and receive a full refund on all unmailed benefits.

OR Make check or money order payable to A.R.E. (Non-U.S. residents must make payment in United States funds.)

☐ Check or Money Order ☐ MasterCard ☐ VISA

If payment is enclosed, please use envelope for your privacy.

Expiration Date | Charge Card Number

Mo. | Yr.

1712

Signature_____
(Important! Sign here to use credit card.)

Name *(please print)* _____

Address _____

City_____ State _____ Zip _____

Phone   (_____) _____

☐ I can't join right now, but please send me additional information about A.R.E. activities, publications, and membership.

How Can I Participate in A.R.E.?

Although A.R.E. Headquarters is located in Virginia Beach, Virginia–where visitors are always welcome– the A.R.E. is a global network of individuals in more than seventy countries. The underlying principle of the Edgar Cayce readings is the oneness of all life, tolerance for all people, and a compassion and understanding for individuals of all faiths, races, and backgrounds.

In addition to Headquarters, hundreds of study groups and Edgar Cayce Centers exist world-wide. Regardless of your location, individuals are invited to participate in group activities, explore new publications, or simply enjoy membership benefits through the mail.

For additional information about the organization's activities and services, please use the card below or contact:

A.R.E., 67th Street & Atlantic Ave.
P.O. Box 595, Virginia Beach, VA 23451-0595

The Wealth of Insights Contained in the Edgar Cayce Material Includes:

Alternative Healing Principles	*Universal Laws*	*Global Community*
Dreams	*Attitudes & Emotions*	*ESP*
Spiritual Healing	*Mysticism*	*Self-Hypnosis*
Study Groups	*Karma & Grace*	*Death & Dying*
Earth Changes	*Meditation*	*Prophecy*
Psychic Development	*Spiritual Guidance*	*Astrology*
Atlantis & Ancient Civilizations	*Reincarnation*	*Akashic Records*
Discovering Your Soul's Purpose	*Angels*	*And Hundreds More...*

EDGAR CAYCE FOUNDATION and
A.R.E. LIBRARY/VISITORS CENTER
Virginia Beach, Virginia
Serving You Since 1931

NO POSTAGE
NECESSARY
IF MAILED
IN THE
UNITED STATES

BUSINESS REPLY MAIL
FIRST CLASS MAIL PERMIT NO. 2456, VIRGINIA

POSTAGE WILL BE PAID BY ADDRESSEE

A.R.E.®

P.O. Box 595

Virginia Beach, VA 23451-9909